Troy Chronicles
Stories of an American City

Don Rittner

New Netherland Press
Schenectady, N.Y.

Dedicated To

Olivia, Sophia, Miriya, Kayleigh and Logan

Make history kids!

©2016 Don Rittner

All Rights Reserved. No part of this publication may be reproduced or transmitted in any form or by and means, electronic or mechanical, except brief quotes extracted for the purpose of book reviews or similar articles, with the permission in writing from the author.

First American paperback edition 2016.

ISBN-10:0-9624263-7-7
ISBN-13:978-0-9624263-7-7

Table of Contents

Dedication
Acknowledgements
Introduction, 1

Chapter One
Sports, 3

Troy's Knockout History-Round One, 3

Chapter Two
The Civil War, 13

Slavery Not Tolerated Here!, 13
Troy's Ironclad History, 19
The Battle Of Hampton Roads, 23
Uncle Sam's Uncle Tom, 27
Underground Railroad Stopped Here, 31
Don't Know "Jack" About History?, 35
Troy's "Monitor Boys", 39

Chapter Three
Art, 43

Famous Historic Painting Of Troy Has Wrong Troy Location, 43
Rare Drawing Of Troy Finally Identified, 49

Chapter Four
Culture, 57

Hollywood On The Hudson, 57
Play It Again, Helen, 61
Hollywood Via Troy Part One, 65
Hollywood Via Troy Part Two, 69

'Twas The Night Before Christmas, 73
Will The Real Helen Stand Up!, 77
Helen Of Troy, N.Y. - Act II, 81
Will Troy's Proctor's Finally Be Saved, 85
Twas The Night Before Christmas Began In Troy, 97

Chapter Five
Music, 101

Manhattan Transfer And The Troy Connection, 101
Frankie Carle And The Troy Brothel, 109

Chapter Six
The Law, 111

Troy's Early Law & Order, 111
Troy's First "Copps," 115
Double Trouble In '82, 119
"Community Police" Not New, 122

Troy Chronicles

Introduction

"Trojans are the most enterprising persevering, go-ahead set of fellows in the world."
- Philip Hone, 1835

Troy, New York is a city on the Hudson River not far from where the Mohawk River meets and forms the Hudson-Mohawk Gateway, a region that allows passage from north to south and east to west through New York State. It is where these two mighty rivers join that provided a suitable location for the rise of one of the most innovative cities of the 19th century.

What began as a Dutch farmstead rose to become an industrial giant during the 19th century. It was partly due to location of two excellent powerful streams - the Wynantskill and Poestenkill - for power, along with a determined population, many of which immigrated from New England during the so called "Yankee Invasion" of the 1790s. They sought out their dreams and fortunes on the newly laid out village of Vanderheyden, later renamed Troy.

The impact of this city on the United States during the 19th century was enormous. Thousands of bells were cast and supplied the righteous tones to a growing nation of religious believers. Thousands of cast iron stoves made in Troy heated those churches, homes, and businesses. Horses provided their power wearing Burden Troy made horseshoes. Steam locomotives rode over the Troy-made rails, and naval history was even changed as the U.S.S. Monitor during the Civil War outgunned the confederate ship Merrimac wearing Troy-made skin of iron. Nine of ten men wore collars, cuffs, and shirts made mostly by the female population of the city that by 1920 outnumbered the males living in the city.

Troy Chronicles

It isn't all about industry even if more than 130 patents were issued to Trojans from 1790 to 1850. Trojans provided their skill sets in the arts, entertainment, science, education, and a host of other pursuits.

This collection of 25 essays deals with Trojans that have contributed in sports, the Civil War, art, culture, music, and the law. It is an eclectic collection picked from a series of weekly articles I wrote for the Troy Record newspaper from 1999 to 2005. Its purpose is to give you a flavor for the types of people that made Troy great over its two centuries of history. The year 2016 marks the Bicentennial of the incorporation of the city and this book is an honor to those two centuries of history.

You can reach me at drittner@aol.com.

Or on Facebook at www.facebook.com/drittner

All illustrations are from the Library of Congress, public domain, or unless otherwise specified. Please send errors and corrections to my email address.

Don Rittner
July 2016

Chapter One
SPORTS

TROY'S KNOCKOUT HISTORY-ROUND ONE

Did You Know?

1. Troy's Paddy Ryan won the first true Heavyweight Championship of the World from the English champion Joe Goss on May 30, 1880.

2. Troy's John Morrissey won the Heavyweight Championship of America on October 12, 1853, against Yankee Sullivan (James Ambrose, alias Frank Murray). He is better known for creating the Saratoga Racetrack.

The "sport" of boxing has been around for a very long time. There is evidence of fist fighting as a sport in Ethiopia about 6,000 years ago. It eventually spread to Egypt and throughout the Mediterranean region. Even ancient Crete had a boxing-like sport around 1,500 B.C.

In Greece, two Greek boxers sat on stones facing each other and pounded away until one of them was knocked out. Fighters did wear leather thongs to protect their hands and wrists, but as it progressed, these thongs turned into weapons as harder leather was used. There were no breaks in the fighting either.

Troy Chronicles

The Greeks introduced the sport into the Olympic Games, complete with rules, back in 688 BC. However, the Olympics were also performed in the nude, so better to have rules than not.

The Roman Empire continued the boxing tradition - sort of - and invented the boxing ring, a circle drawn in the sand or platform. Now you know why today's square boxing platform is called the "ring."

The Roman form of the sport was more like their gladiator events -- often brutal in comparison to the Greeks. They created the Caestus, a leather wrapping with iron and brass studs obviously designed to inflict pain. That wasn't painful enough for them so they created the bronze Myrmex (which means limb piercer). Since they were using slaves to fight the contests, it was more like a Fox weekend special - a fight to the death entertainment show - than boxing, as we know it today. Rome eventually banned the limb piercer and boxing altogether around 30 BC.

After Rome fell, it would take more than 1000 years before the sport was reintroduced - by the English, no less.

It was an illiterate Englishmen, James Figg, the first heavyweight champion in the sport's history, who opened a fight academy in London in 1719, and made boxing popular (he was also a fencer, so was "respectable").

Yet, it would take another 24 years before the well-educated Jack Broughton, considered the "Father of English Boxing," wrote the first British boxing rules. These rules outlawed hitting below the belt, or hitting an opponent that was down. Wrestling holds were allowed but only above the waist.

Under Broughton's rules, there was a 3-foot square in the center of the ring and when a fighter was knocked down, his handlers had 30 seconds to pick him up and position him on one side of the square, or the fight was over.

Broughton is given credit for inventing the first boxing gloves, called "mufflers," but they were used only in practice, not in a real fight.

These rules were used throughout England with only minor tampering until the Pugilistic Society (founded in 1814) developed the London Prize Ring Rules in 1838.

The new rules called for a ring 24 feet square, enclosed by two ropes. A knockdown marked the end of a round. Rounds were introduced with a 30 second break. The fighters were given eight seconds to "toe the mark," or "come to scratch," unaided, in the center of the ring after the break or the fight was over.

English rules were used until 1889 when the last bare-knuckle championship bout was fought.

Boxing first began in America between black slaves whose masters' wagered huge sums against them. The first great American fighter, a slave named Tom Molineaux, won his freedom by knocking out a champ from a rival plantation. In 1809, he went to England to fight and won a couple of fights. In 1810-1811 he fought and lost to the English champion Tom Cribb. His jaw was broken on the last fight.

Bill Richmond the "Black Terror" of Staten Island was a servant of General Lord Percy, who commanded the British forces occupying New York during the Revolution. Richmond fought a number of British soldiers and never lost. Percy took him to England to fight in 1777.

Richmond knocked out his first English opponent in 25 seconds. In 1805, he too was knocked out by British champion Tom Cribb. He was 41 years old. Richmond continued fighting until he was 52 and never lost again.

Most fighting in America was frowned upon or even made illegal in the Eastern part of the country, so many fights were held in the Midwest to escape the law. It wasn't until after the Civil War that boxing came into its own. Credit is given to the Boston boxer John L. Sullivan and the Queensbury Rules for making the sport popular and acceptable here.

In 1866, the Marquis of Queensbury, a big supporter in British sporting circles, laid down a new set of rules. These rules included the mandatory wearing of gloves. Unlike the English rules that dealt with bare knuckle, there was no wrestling allowed at all. Rounds were three minutes with a one-minute rest period between. Finally a boxer had ten seconds to recover from a knockdown. These are the basic rules we follow today.

John L. Sullivan (1858-1918), the "Boston Strong Boy," became the first great sports hero in America and began his rise in fame by beating Troy's Paddy Ryan which is known in boxing circles as the first great prize fight in American boxing history. Sullivan was known as an honest fighter. He would fight anyone (but refused to fight black men), anywhere, with bare fists, skintight or padded gloves, and under any rules.

He is credited with saying, *"I will fight any man breathing. Always on the level, yours truly, John L. Sullivan."*

Troy has a unique place in the early history of American Boxing with three fighters, Paddy Ryan, John Morrissey, and John C. Heenan. All three were bare-knuckle fighters and two of them (Ryan and Morrissey) were heavyweight champions of America.

For the working class, living in Troy during the 19th century often meant using your fists to get by.

Troy Chronicles

The infamous 'Watervliet Cut' a lateral part of the Erie Canal that allowed access to Troy, was lined with saloons, and one writer reported that bodies were found floating in that portion of the canal way too often. Troy's first boxing champion ran one of those saloons.

Patrick Henry (Paddy) Ryan (1851-1900)

Paddy Ryan, known as the Trojan Giant was born in Thurles, Tipperary, Ireland on March 14, 1851, but lived in Troy, West Troy, and Green Island. Standing at 5 foot 11 inches (some

PADDY RYAN,
Ex-Champion Heavy-Weight Pugilist of America.

reports are 6 foot 1 1/2 inches), he weighed in at 195-200 pounds.

It has been written that Ryan was a better wrestler than boxer but he certainly did like to fight. He opened his famous saloon at the Sidecut around 1874. His ease at dealing with "problems" impressed Jimmy Killoran, athletic director at the Rensselaer Polytechnic Institute. Taking Ryan under his wing, Ryan was ready for professional boxing by 1877.

On May 30, 1880, Paddy won the first true Heavyweight Championship of the World from Joe Goss, the English champion, at Coillier's Station, West Virginia in the 87th round (after fighting an hour and a half).

Paddy lost it two years later, on February 7th, fighting John L. Sullivan, the Boston Strong Boy (bare knuckled and under London Prize Ring rules) in nine rounds. Ryan reportedly said Sullivan, a powerful right-handed puncher, *"Hit me like he held a telegraph pole."*

Ryan and Sullivan liked to fight each other. Between January 19, 1885 and February 17, 1897, Sullivan fought Paddy at least a dozen times, Sullivan winning all the matches.

Ryan died on December 14, 1900, in a rented house on Albany Avenue, Green Island and was buried in St. Mary's Cemetery in that village. He was elected to the Ring Boxing Hall of Fame in 1973.

John Morrissey (1831-1878)

John Morrissey, known as "Old Smoke," was born in Templemore, Tipperary County, Ireland on February 5, 1831, but was raised by an immigrant Irish family in Troy. He stood close to 6 foot tall and weighed in at 170-176 pounds.

Morrissey got his nickname 'Old Smoke' from a battle against a Native American named Tom McCann. Morrissey was pinned on his back over burning coals from a stove that had been knocked over in the bout. While steam and smoke and the smell of burning flesh permeated from Morrissey, he continued to fight without notice. This came as a surprise of the crowd that expected him to call "Enough," the signal to surrender.

Troy Chronicles

Morrissey didn't have many fights, but he did win the Heavyweight Championship of America on October 12, 1853, at Boston Corners, NY, on the border of Massachusetts and New York, against Yankee Sullivan (James Ambrose, alias Frank Murray). Sullivan apparently won the fight and beat Morrissey badly, but left the ring and ignored the "Time" call so the referee declared Morrissey the winner.

Morrissey upheld his Heavyweight title to Troy's John C. Heenan on October 20, 1858, at Long Point, Canada. Heenan actually broke his right hand early on in the fight and fought at a disadvantage. Morrissey gave up the heavyweight championship and retired from the ring.

Morrissey was known as a strong, tough, fighter but had little boxing acumen. After retiring from the ring, he became a prominent politician and served two terms in the United States Congress and twice in the New York State Senate.

Morrissey is probably better known for creating the Saratoga Racetrack.

He opened gambling operations in Saratoga for the summer spa season in the 1860s and opened his soon to become world famous Clubhouse in 1870. He began the horse racing course in the late 1860s. Morrissey was a pioneer in using the newly invented telegraph to make betting available to everyone.

He died on May 1, 1878, at the Adelphi Hotel in Saratoga at age 47 just after his election (he won, against Tammany Hall's handpicked candidate in the wealthiest election district in New York City) and was buried in Saratoga. The New York State Legislature closed on the day of his burial and the entire elected body attended funeral services in Troy. An estimated crowd of 12,000 stood outside the church to pay tribute to the American Champion.

Troy Chronicles

He was elected to the Ring Boxing Hall of Fame in 1954.

John Camel Heenan (1835-1873)

John Camel Heenan was the only one of the three actually born in Troy on May 2, 1835. He was raised by an immigrant Irish family also. Heenan stood 6 foot 2 inches and weighed in at 182-195 pounds. He was known as the Benicia Boy, from swinging a sledgehammer in the Pacific Mail Steamship Company's Benicia, California repair works.

Heenan fought John Morrissey for the Heavyweight Championship of America in 1858, but broke his right hand early in the fight hitting a ring stake and fought at a disadvantage.

Heenan was the first American boxer known to lift weights and punch bags as part of his training regimen for a bout with the English champion Thomas Sayers. On April 17, 1860, in Hampshire, England, Heenan fought the five foot eight inch, 154-pound Sayers. Sayers fractured his right arm in the 6th round from a hit by Heenan. Constables tried to stop the fight in the 36th round after two hours, but spectators were pushed into the ring. They fought five more rounds before it was finally declared a draw. Champion belts were made for both fighters.

Heenan was known as a clever boxer with "tremendous punching power," but was probably better known for marrying Adah Isaacs Menken, a famous San Francisco actress of the time who was the notorious, glamorous, beautiful, and infamous "Mazeppa," a play based on the poem of Lord Byron. Heenan made a practice of beating Adah every night after dinner. So she divorced him. She married five times.

Heenan toured around the country with Englishman "Gypsy" Jem Mace, the 'Father of Modern Boxing' giving exhibitions.

He died at Green River Station, Wyoming Territory on November 2, 1873, and was buried in St Agnes Cemetery in Menands.

The Benicia Boy was elected to the Ring Boxing Hall of Fame in 1954.

Troy Chronicles

Chapter Two
THE CIVIL WAR

SLAVERY NOT TOLERATED HERE!

Did You Know?

1. Under the Dutch, slaves could purchase their freedom, own land, start a business, and become members of the Dutch Reformed Church.

2. Thirty years before we fought the Civil War, there were no slaves in the Capital District.

3. In the Capital District, slaves were set free (called manumission) as early as 1795.

"SLAVERY! How much misery is comprehended in that single word"
--Henry Highland Garnet, 16 August 1843.

Slavery is a crime against humanity that rates high on the dumb list along with genocide and "ethnic cleansing." Unfortunately, slavery was practiced in this country for many years before the Civil War.

Slavery was introduced in New York in 1626 when 11 blacks were brought in for forced labor.

When the federal government conducted its first census in 1790, there were 1,474 slaveholding families in Albany County owning 3,722 slaves. At least 23 of those families had

Troy Chronicles

10-19 slaves each. Rensselaer County was part of Albany County until 1791.

By 1800, Rensselaer County had 890 slaves, decreasing to 750 in 1810, 433 in 1820, and by 1830, none. Slavery was abolished in the State in 1827.

On the reverse, there were 632 free slaves living here in 1820 rising to 1,058 free slaves before the Civil War began.

So, for thirty years before we fought the Civil War, there were no slaves in the Capital District.

Many people, especially in the northern states, believed it was wrong to own another human being. The abolitionist movement during the three decades before the Civil War made the slavery question the prime concern of national politics and quickened the demise of slavery in America. But the end of slavery began much earlier.

In 1774, Connecticut and Rhode Island banned importation of slaves. In 1776, Society of Friends (Quakers) abolished slavery among its members. The following year, Vermont prohibited slavery. By 1780, Massachusetts adopted a freedom clause interpreted as prohibiting slavery. Pennsylvania adopted gradual emancipation. In 1784, Connecticut and Rhode Island passed gradual emancipation laws. Four years later, Connecticut prohibited residents from participating in slave trade.

On March 29, 1799, New York State passed a gradual emancipation law declaring that after July 4, 1799, every child born to a slave within the state would be free, although he/she would remain with the owner, mother, executors, or assigns until the age of 28 if male, or 25 if female. Every black person born before July 4, 1799, was free after July 4, 1827.

Troy Chronicles

However, in the Capital District, slaves were set free (called manumission) as early as 1795. Elkanah Watson freed one of his slaves, Sarah March, and recorded the deed in the minutes of the Town of Watervliet. Many other manumissions are recorded as well from other slaveholders.

Troy played an important role as part of the Underground Railroad, a loosely formed network of whites, free slaves, and anyone else sympathetic to smuggling southern slaves to Canada or other Northern U.S. States. It actually began during the colonial period as a reaction to the Fugitive Slave Act of 1793. This act provided for the return of escaped black slaves between states.

The law was hardly enforced in the North since slavery was being abolished, but as a concession to the South a second and stronger fugitive slave law was passed as part of the Compromise of 1850. This law was tested in Troy ten years later.

In November 1834, the Liberty Street Presbyterian Church was being dedicated on the north side of Liberty Street between Third and Fourth Streets. Its new pastor, The Rev. Henry Highland Garnet was brought in from Oberlin College, staying for several years. While Garnet was here, he formulated strong anti-slavery views. Garnet delivered a "Call to Rebellion at the National Negro Convention in Buffalo, New York, in 1843, encouraging African-Americans to resist slavery by means of armed rebellion. At the party convention for the Liberty Party in Buffalo, Garnet served on the nominating committee while African-Americans participated directly for the first time.

The abolitionist movement took off in the 1830's, partly as a result of the evangelical movement that swept the north starting in the 1820's. It not only called for the end of slavery but also called for women's rights. By 1838, more than 1,350 antislavery societies existed with almost 250,000 members, including many women.

Uncle Tom's Cabin, by Harriet Beecher Stowe, which became an effective piece of abolitionist propaganda was first performed in America in Troy, in 1852, in Peale's Museum on the corner of Fulton and River Street.

The jail where Charles Nalle was held lies below First and State Streets.

Troy Chronicles

The fugitive slave acts were detested. When a runaway slave was captured, he or she was taken before a Federal court or commissioner, denied a jury trial and his/her testimony was not admitted. Only the statement of the master claiming ownership, even if absent, was taken as the main evidence.

Obviously unfair, new personal-liberty laws contradicting the legislation of 1850 were passed in most of the Northern states. Abolitionists openly defied the 1850 act.

The northern newspapers have several episodes where citizens took it upon themselves to help runaway slaves. More than 1,000 soldiers had to be used to guard escaped Virginia slave Anthony Burns in Boston when Bostonians failed to free him after they stormed the federal courthouse. A riot broke out in Lancaster County, Pennsylvania, when a federal official ordered Quaker bystanders to help catch a runaway - they didn't"t. The Quakers were prosecuted, but not convicted.

In Troy, we have the famous case of Charles Nalle. Nalle was a coachman for Uri Gilbert, Troy businessman and later Mayor. At the age of 28, he escaped from the plantation master Blucher W. Hasbrough of Culpepper County, Virginia, on October 19th, 1848. He made it to our area and first worked for William Scram at Sand Lake as a teamster. He told his secret to Horace F. Averill, a lawyer in Sand Lake who notified Hasbrough. Nalle was arrested on April 27, 1860 and brought to the U.S. Commissioners office on the second floor at the corner of First and State. Several hundred people waited for Nalle to be brought out and rescued him, taking him to the woods in Niskayuna, and later Amsterdam, before they eventually bought his freedom for $650. He returned to Troy a free man.

Civilization is a great concept and someday humanity may achieve it.

Officers on deck (left to right): Robinson W. Hands from Troy, 3rd Asst. Engineer; Louis N. Stodder, Albert B. Campbell (seated), William Flye (with binoculars). Note dents in turret from cannon fire. (Photo courtesy U.S. Navy) Below officers on deck.

TROY'S IRONCLAD HISTORY

DID YOU KNOW?

1. THE USS MONITOR WAS PERSONALLY FINANCED BY TROY BUSINESSMEN.

2. THE IRON HULL PLATES WERE MADE IN TROY.

3. ONLY THE FACADE OF THE ALBANY ROLLING MILL, WHICH MADE THE HULL PLATES, STILL STANDS.

The city of Troy played a pivotal role in turning the Civil War in favor of the Union. Many of our factories produced material for the war effort. W. & L.E. Gurley made brass fuses for bombs; Corning, Winslow & Co. made steel rifled cannons; Eaton, Gilbert & Co. made army wagons; Burden Iron Company made horseshoes; Sweet, Quimby & Co. made shot and shells; F.W. Parmener made ammo wagons; Jones & Co. made brass cannons; and casting mortar shells were made by both Fuller, Warren and Co. and Knight, Harrison & Paine.

However, it was two of South Troy's iron manufacturers, the Rensselaer and Albany Iron works, that made machinery and plates for the Union's first ironclad warship, the Monitor, a ship that changed naval history forever. Furthermore, if it wasn't for the patriotism and political connections of the owners of those iron works, John A Griswold and John F. Winslow, the Monitor may never have seen the light of day.

It was the famous battle between the Monitor and the South's Virginia (Merrimac) on the morning of March 9, 1862 at Hampton Roads, Virginia, that most historians consider the turning of the tide for the Union. The Monitor battled the Merrimac to a standstill taking away the naval advantage that

Troy Chronicles

John Ericsson, designer of the USS Monitor.

the Confederacy enjoyed for a brief time.

Learning that the South was developing iron ships, the US Navy's newly created Ironclad Board, placed ads in Northern newspapers on August 3, 1861, inviting designers to submit plans for the construction of ironclad warships.

John Ericsson, a Swedish inventor who became an American citizen in 1848, wrote a letter to Abraham Lincoln on August 29th offering to build an ironclad vessel in 90 days. However, Ericsson, a brilliant engineer, inventor of air compressors, boilers, engines, locomotives, naval guns and the screw propeller, was at odds with the Navy after an accident in 1844 in which one of his cannon designs blew up killing both the Secretary of the Navy, Secretary of State, and others.
As luck would have it, Ericsson received a visit from Cornelius Bushnell, of New Haven, Connecticut who sought out the inventor's expertise on a matter of an ironclad ship he was going to build called the Galena. Ericsson asked Bushnell to look at a model of his Monitor.

Ericsson had originally submitted his design for a "cupola battery" to Emperor Napoleon III several years before the Franco-Russian War, but it was graciously declined. Ericsson also was not new to iron ships having designed and built them in Europe in the 1830's.

Bushnell offered to take the model and plan to Washington on the inventor's behalf and present it to the Naval Board.

Troy Chronicles

He presented the model to Troy's Griswold and Winslow and explained the properties of the vessel that Ericsson had given him. With their help, a letter of introduction was obtained from the Governor of New York and delivered to Lincoln, on Bushnell's behalf. The three men, Bushnell, Winslow and Griswold, went to pitch the Naval board.

The President accompanied the three men to the Navy Department where they met with the Navy Board on September 13, 1861. It was a tough sell to the board since some Navy folks still had a grudge against Ericsson. Before Lincoln left the meeting he had the final word that day. He was holding the model studying its unique features and remarked, *"All I have to say is what the girl said when she stuck her foot in the stocking. It strikes me there's something in it!"*

Winslow or Bushnell decided to get Ericsson to present the final case himself. He did and got the go ahead to build the ship in 100 days. Griswold, Winslow, and Bushnell were guarantors of the project.

Ericsson immediately went to work. He contracted with Thomas Fitch Rowland, proprietor of the Continental Iron Works in Greenpoint, Long Island (Brooklyn) to build the battery.

The ship was 172 feet long with a 41 foot 6 inch beam. Two 12-inch guns would be housed in a revolving turret. The ship would have a flat deck with only 18 inches of free board and a draft of 10 feet 6 inches. This would allow the ship to easily operate and maneuver in any of the South's inland waters.

The majority of the iron plates, bolts, nuts, and rivets were manufactured in New York State. Holdane & Company, the Albany Iron Works, and the Rensselaer Iron Works provided tons of flat plates, and angle iron. The Niagara Steam Forge pounded out the eight-inch thick port stoppers. The turret and machinery were made at the Novelty Iron Works.

Troy Chronicles

Back in the early 1980's, workers at the old Iron Works (then Portec) showed me a few extra Monitor hull plates they had in store. The Mohawk Hudson Gateway now has those in possession.

The iron turret had an interior diameter of 20 feet. The eight layers of one-inch thick plate were assembled around an iron skeleton. The structure was powered by two "donkey engines" that turned massive gears and provided the turret with 2 1/2 rpm. The turret revolved on a brass ring set into the deck and a shaft from below raised up by a wedge and set to put the turret in motion. When Ericsson learned that the Navy had no 12-inch guns ready, he recalculated to incorporate two XI inch Dahlgren smoothbore cannons.

The public was not impressed. Local papers began printing articles about "Ericsson's Folly" and how the ship would slide to the bottom of the East River when launched.

On January 20th, 1862, Ericsson wrote to Secretary Fox proposing the name of the ship be the Monitor. Ten days later, on January 30, 1862, 101 days after the contract was signed, a ship that was unlike anything the world had seen slid down into the East River at the Continental Iron Works. There were many bystanders who were witness to what they thought would be a slide to the bottom of the river. Ericsson stood on the stern of his ship and when launched it floated to within 3 inches of his designed water line.

The ship was turned over to the Navy Department and commissioned on February 25, 1862. It had devices containing over 40 original patents on board including a flush toilet. The USS Monitor steamed for Hampton Roads on March 6, 1862 and on the morning of March 9, 1862 entered the annals of history forever.

Troy Chronicles

THE BATTLE OF HAMPTON ROADS

Did You Know?

1. Two of the hull plates made for the Monitor still survive and can be seen in the Burden Museum in South Troy.

2. The area of the Battle of Hampton Road was full of Trojans. Trojans were on the Monitor, in Fortress Monroe, and above the area in a hot air balloon doing aerial reconnaissance. Fortress Monroe was under the command of Troy's General John Wool.

During the Civil War, the Union began the building of 76 ironclad war ships, commissioning 42 of them before May 1, 1865.

On the Confederate side, 59 ironclads were started, but only 24 were completed.

Very few Civil War ironclads were sunk by gunfire. Instead, the Confederate ironclads were purposely destroyed to prevent capture by Union forces. Of the total of 66 ironclads on both sides combined, only 12 were actually sunk by the enemy in battle.

None of them developed the legend like the battle between the Union's Monitor, parts of which were built in Troy, and the Virginia, also known as the Merrimac.

On the afternoon of March 8, 1862, a naval battle occurred that changed naval warfare forever. The first Confederate ironclad steamed down the Elizabeth River into Hampton Roads, Virginia to attack the wooden-sided U.S. blockading

Troy Chronicles

fleet anchored there. The Virginia, or Merrimac, originally a wooden ship sunk by the Union, but raised by the Confederates and converted into an ironclad ship, attacked the Union Navy fleet, comprising several ships armed with 204 guns and aided by land batteries.

By six o'clock, the sole Virginia had sunk the Cumberland, burned the Congress, forced the Minnesota ashore, and forced the St. Lawrence and the Roanoke to seek shelter under the guns of Fort Monroe. It left the Union fleet in shambles with plans on returning the next day to finish the job. The results of the first day's fighting at Hampton Roads proved the superiority of iron over wood, but on the next day it was to be iron vs. iron as the U.S.S. Monitor arrived on the scene.

On March 9, the Virginia was greeted by the Monitor, an ironclad more heavily armored, with a revolving gun turret, and speedier and more agile in the water due to the inventive genius of its designer John Ericsson.

Monitor Captain John L. Worden.

For four to five hours the two ironclads battered each other, until a shell from the Virginia exploded on the eye-slit of Monitor's pilot house, blinding the commander, Captain John L. Worden. Both ships retreated thinking they had won.

Troy Chronicles

Troy's Major General John E. Wool, commander of Fort Monroe.

Lieutenant S. Dana Greene, an officer aboard Monitor, described the first exchange of gunfire: "The turrets and other parts of the ship were heavily struck, but the shots did not penetrate; the tower was intact, and it continued to revolve. A look of confidence passed over the men's faces, and we believed the Merrimac would not repeat the work she had accomplished the day before."

The next day, a letter was sent to Maj. George McClellan, commander of the Army, from Maj. Gen. John E. Wool, commander of Fort Monroe.

"GENERAL: Two hours after I sent my hurried dispatch to the Secretary of War last evening the Monitor arrived, and saved the Minnesota and the St. Lawrence, which were both aground when she arrived."

Wool, a hero of two previous wars, and also from Troy, fired off another letter to his friend John Griswold and wrote, *"The*

Troy Chronicles

Monitor saved everything inside and outside Fortress Monroe." Clearly both Trojans knew that they had a hand in preventing the further destruction of the Union Navy, clearly giving the win to the North.

It was two Trojans, iron magnates John A Griswold and John F. Winslow, along with inventor John Ericsson, and financier Cornelius Bushnell that made the Monitor a reality. Trojans are very proud of the fact.

During the night of the battle at Hampton Roads, ironworkers who helped make the plates for the Monitor marched by torch light to downtown Troy in celebration. Today, several of the hull plates rolled but not used are on display at the Burden Iron Works Museum in the Burden Office Building operated by the Hudson Mohawk Industrial Gateway in South Troy. The bank room where the finances were developed in the old Manufacturers National Bank of Troy was removed when the old building was demolished on the corner of King and River Streets and reassembled into their new bank building on the corner of Grand and Fourth Streets. The room is still there to see. You can read Wool's quote to Griswold and see a depiction of the famous battle on the statue at Monument Square. Troy made a major contribution to the Civil War. There are several Web sites that show you how to build models of both ships.

There are many first's associated with the USS Monitor. It was the first ship to have a revolving turret. It was the first ship where the officers and crew had to live entirely below waterline, and it was the first ship credited with having below waterline flushing toilets. Finally, the Monitor and its gravesite is the first U.S. National Marine Sanctuary.

Troy Chronicles

UNCLE SAM'S UNCLE TOM

DID YOU KNOW?

1. THE PLAY WAS FIRST PERFORMED IN TROY AND LASTED OVER 100 CONSECUTIVE DAYS.

2. STOWE'S CLASSIC WAS FIRST PUBLISHED AS A SERIES OF MAGAZINE ARTICLES.

3. WHEN ABRAHAM LINCOLN MET STOWE, HE SAID, "SO THIS IS THE LITTLE LADY WHO STARTED THIS GREAT WAR." HE WAS REFERRING TO THE POPULARITY OF HER BOOK.

The book Uncle Tom's Cabin has been often labeled as the kindling wood of the Civil War. Written in 1852 by Harriet Beecher Stowe, a child of a Protestant preacher, it was originally penned as a set of articles for the Washington anti-slavery weekly, the National Era.

The mother of seven children, and a teacher, Stowe wrote to support her family. This included poetry, travel guides, biographies, children's books and adult novels. Yet, her name is forever etched in the annals of those who spoke against slavery during the pre-Civil War period.

Uncle Tom's Cabin peaked public interest on the subject of slavery, but it was also based on Stowe's life experiences growing up next to the slave state Kentucky. She had firsthand knowledge about slavery, the anti-slavery movement, and the Underground Railroad, a network to help slaves escape to the north.

The book aroused intense controversy and made Stowe a national celebrity. To help dispel the attacks on her work, she published A Key to Uncle Tom's Cabin the following year documenting the book's truths. She followed up with another anti-slavery novel, "Dred" in 1856. When meeting President Lincoln in 1862, he is reported to have greeted her as "the little lady who made this Great War."

The first public performance of Uncle Tom's Cabin occurred in Troy on September 27, 1852, on the stage of Peale's Museum, corner of Fulton and River Streets. It was a family production, mostly relatives of actor George C. Howard, and the museum manager. His wife Caroline, four-year-old daughter Cordelia, and George himself played major characters. George Aiken, Howard's cousin penned the dramatic version. Another of the actors was William J. Le Moyne, who later went on to become a national stage star specializing in Dickens's works.

Harriet Beecher Stowe.

Troy Chronicles

The Auction scene, 1901.

The script ran three hours and fifteen minutes, but only took the story up through little Eva's death. In November, Aiken rewrote and ended it with Stowe's finale. The two scripts were combined that month into a drama of six acts that became the standard acting version of the play. It was so popular in Troy; it ran for 150 consecutive nights.

The play was performed continuously in the United States for eighty years. The Howard's appeared in Uncle Tom's Cabin until 1857 when Howard undertook the management of the Troy Adelphi Theater, but the season failed and George, Caroline, and Cordelia went on the road eventually managing a New York theater. Cordelia retired at age thirteen.

Twenty years before Stowe's book was published and the play performed, the anti-slavery sentiment was in full swing in Troy. Slavery was no stranger to residents of Troy, but was abolished in New York in 1827. By 1830, there were no slaves living in Rensselaer County.

In November 1834, the Liberty Street Presbyterian Church at Liberty Street between Third and Fourth Streets gained a new pastor, Rev. Henry Highland Garnet. Garnet was a leading abolitionist. His "Call to Rebellion" at the National Negro Convention in Buffalo, New York, in 1843, encouraged African-Americans to resist slavery by means of armed rebellion. It gained him national attention.

The abolitionist movement took off in the 1830's, partly as a result of the evangelical movement that swept the north during the previous decade. It called for the end of slavery and promoted women's rights. By 1838, more than 1,350 antislavery societies existed with almost 250,000 members, including many women.

Captured runaways were taken before a Federal court or commissioner and denied a jury trial. Only the statement of the master, even if absent, was taken as the main evidence. Many people did not like this injustice and some participated in the Underground Railroad movement.

Not only was the Underground Railroad alive and well in Troy, it wasn't always underground. Our famous example is the case of Charles Nalle, a coachman for Uri Gilbert, Troy businessman and Mayor.

On October 19th, 1848, the 28-year-old Nalle escaped from his plantation master Blucher W. Hasbrough of Culpepper County, Virginia. He worked for William Scram at Sand Lake as a teamster, but told his secret to Horace F. Averill, a lawyer in Sand Lake who notified Hasbrough.

Nalle was arrested on April 27, 1860, and brought to the U.S. Commissioners office on the second floor of a bank at the northeast corner of First and State Streets. Several hundred people, including Harriet Tubman who was on her way to Boston, waited for Nalle to be brought out and rescued him. His freedom was purchased for $650 and returned to Troy a free man.

Troy Chronicles

UNDERGROUND RAILROAD STOPPED HERE

DID YOU KNOW?

1. THE STEPHEN AND HARRIET MYERS RESIDENCE IS NOW OWNED BY THE UNDERGROUND RAILROAD HISTORY PROJECT OF THE CAPITAL DISTRICT IN ALBANY, NY AND IS UNDERTAKING IT'S RESTORATION.

2. THE UNDERGROUND RAILROAD WAS ANYTHING BUT UNDERGROUND. ABOLITIONISTS WERE WELL KNOWN IN THE COMMUNITY.

3. HENRY HIGHLAND GARNET IN THE 1840S GAINED A NATIONAL AND INTERNATIONAL REPUTATION AS AN ANTI-SLAVERY REFORMER AT THE LIBERTY STREET PRESBYTERIAN CHURCH.

> *This is a world of compensations; and he who would be no slave must consent to have no slave. Those who deny freedom to others deserve it not for themselves.*
> -Abraham Lincoln

Henry Highland Garnet in the 1840s gained a national and international reputation as an anti-slavery reformer at the Liberty Street Presbyterian Church.

Troy Chronicles

Henry Highland Garnet.

The Underground Railroad, a network of pro-active people opposed to slavery prior to the Civil War was quite active in the Capital District. The area was a major location for helping funnel runaway slaves north to their freedom.

While many in the UGRR did their work behind the scenes, research from groups like Albany's Underground Railroad History Project and others are revealing that many of the participants were quite "public" about their work.

Several people locally participated in the UGRR movement as individuals or members of anti-slavery groups called 'vigilance committees' and all walks of life participated.

Albanians include Rev. John Sands of the Second Wesleyan Church (African); Edward Delavan, owner, Delavan House; William Topp, black tailor; Dr. Thomas Elkins, black pharmacist; Minos McGowan, lumber merchant; Lydia and Abigail Mott, Quaker sisters; Captain Abraham Johnson, black ferry boat operator; barber William Henry Johnson and Stephen Myers, both black, and others.

Myers published the Northern Star and Freeman's Advocate, an arm of the Northern Star Association, a vigilance committee, and it appears he became the local leader of UGRR operations.

The Rev. Able Brown from Sand Lake published the Tocsin of Liberty (Albany Patriot) and listed the slaves he helped free (over a 1,000). Rev. Charles T. Torrey assisted. Torrey, a white abolitionist became a martyr after a trial in 1844, dying in jail in 1846.

A letter carried by a runaway from Brown, which he signed as "cor Secy of Eastern N.Y. A slavery Socy," to his Vermont friend Charles Hicks, a UGRR operator near Bennington, says it all:

"Dear Sir, Please receive the Bearer as a friend who needs your aid and direct him on his way if you cannot give him work he come to us well recommended was a slave a few weeks since."

Albany's Gen. William L. Chaplin was also an agent of the New York Anti-Slavery Society. Chaplin took over Torrey's job as local correspondent of the Albany Patriot and UGRR conductor. In 1850, he was arrested in Rockville, Maryland with two other men who had been held in slavery by members of the US Congress from Georgia. Chaplin was held on bail and married Theodosia Gilbert, business partner of James Caleb Jackson, while incarcerated. He escaped north after friends posted bail. Gilbert's partner, James Caleb Jackson, was the editor of the Albany Patriot and the Liberty Press, both abolitionist papers.

Another UGRR engineer was a Jesuit priest who served Albany and Troy, named John J. Kelley. He is credited with writing the following broadside around 1850:

"We call on our fellow citizens, here and elsewhere, to aid us in funds to help the poor, unfortunate fugitives who come to us daily, in many cases destitute of clothing, weary of traveling and hungry, We appeal to the sympathy of ladies and gentlemen everywhere. We are in want of

Troy Chronicles

material aid and cast off clothing. All funds forwarded to Stephen Myers, William H. Topp, or any gentleman of the committee will be faithfully applied. All letters directed to this office will be duly answered."

This broadside also stated that 287 fugitives were helped through Albany in the ten months prior to July 15, 1856. It also listed the members of the committee as well as an address of the group.

The vigilance committee kept watch for "slave catchers" or "man hunters" coming into the area looking for runaways. Members would let the fugitives know that the hunters were in the area. Many who were working on farms or in businesses would then go into hiding.

There is less known about UGRR activities in Rensselaer County, In addition to Father Kelley, there was the Rev. Fayette Shipherd. Shipherd (1797-1878) and his brother John Jay Shipherd (1802-1844) were Congregational ministers and active abolitionists.

Shipherd in a letter to the same Charles Hicks in Vermont suggests strongly that the Champlain Canal was a northern route to Canada from Troy. In 1842 he writes, *"As the canal has closed I shall send my Southern friends along your road & patronize your house."* He further stares: *"We had 22 (slaves) in two weeks 13 in the city at one time."*

Henry Highland Garnet, a Troy resident in the 1840s gained a national and international reputation as an anti-slavery reformer at the Liberty Street Presbyterian Church.

Also in the Troy area was John H. Hooper, a black fugitive from Maryland. His Troy home served as an UGRR station. The Fox mansion in Sand Lake was a haven for runaways. Researchers have identified more than 60 local sites with UGRR connections.

Troy Chronicles

DON'T KNOW "JACK" ABOUT HISTORY?

Did You Know?

1. Nine men named Jack from Troy worked on making the U.S.S. Monitor.

2. Ironworker John Curley worked the iron with broken bones in his elbow on his right arm, so not to slow down production.

3. Third Engineer Robinson Hands from Troy went down with the ship when it sunk. His bones have not been recovered.

On July 15, 1926, 86-year-old John J. Curley died in his daughter's house at 9 South Burden Avenue in South Troy. It was noted in the local newspapers. "Jack" Curley was the last "survivor" of the nine men involved in making the protective plates for the U.S.S. Monitor at Troy's Albany Iron Works in 1861. Thanks to Schenectady's Ed Curley, Jack Curley will get some better-deserved publicity. Timely too, since the City has allowed the iron works building to be scraped - at the same time our government is spending $7 million to bring up the Monitor's turret and another $30 million for building a Monitor Museum.

Irony is such a fitting word for the next set of facts. There were nine men involved in making the plates for the Monitor. Each of the nine's first name was "John," although they referred to themselves as "Jack."

Troy's John Griswold (then Congressman) and John F. Winslow, owner of the Albany Iron Works, financed the deal, along with John Ericsson who designed the Monitor. Winslow donated the use of the foundry to roll the plates. John Stringham was the foundry's boss roller; John Curley was his helper. John McSurley was the heater; John McDermott was his helper. John Moran was the catcher; John Farrell was the screw tender.

As it turns out, Curley's involvement was not his choosing originally. Curley, an ironworker for the Rensselaer Iron Works, not far from the rolling mill, volunteered for service when the war broke out. Enlisting in Company F of the Second Regiment as a fifer, he was stopped by Boss roller John Stringham who told him he wanted Curley as his assistant in a very special project.

Stringham, Curely, McSurley, McDermott, Moran and Farrell worked day and night in unbearable heat and conditions to make the plates, and with meticulous care, since they had to be perfect in thickness and size. The plates were even shipped to Brooklyn still hot to be placed on the sides of the Monitor.

Interior of the Albany Rolling Mill. It has since burned. Photo by Don Rittner.

Troy Chronicles

They had a deadline of 100 days completion. The plates were made from the best grade Bessemer Steel and each plate was 3 feet wide and 4 to 5 feet long, with a thickness of five eighths of an inch. Each plate weighed 200 pounds.

During one of the rolls, Curley slipped and fell and broke some bones in his elbow on his right arm. Even with a broken arm, he never stopped working the iron. He noticed the pain days later and suffered for the rest of his life.

Those six men worked nine to ten hours a day before taking a rest and it took 30 days to roll the necessary number of plates. Curley, the youngest man on the job, McSurely, Moran and Boss Stringham handled the pouring of the steel from the furnace working with big round balls of hot metal. These balls would run through the rolls back and forth until they were five-eights of an inch thick, and Curley and crew swept them clean getting out scales and impurities with a brush and pail of water. They couldn't afford to make one imperfection and often had to bend over the hot radiating steel. Each plate was as smooth as oilcloth when they were done.

Rensselaer Rolling Mill. It too has burned.

Troy Chronicles

In 1925, the actual rolls that made the plates were standing in the north end of the works. One plate was returned after the battle. It was cracked from a hit from the Virginia (Merrimac). Another clean leftover plate was saved. Both can now be seen in the Hudson Mohawk Industrial Gateway's Burden Museum at the end of Polk Street.

After learning of the defeat of the Virginia, the ironworkers went on a "wet" celebration all night long. Curely remarked that they "felt as if we in Troy had won the battle."

It can be truly said that this decisive battle was indeed a Troy fight. Too bad, there was no fight to save the foundry now being dismantled because of the tunnel vision of the city's planning commission.

One final point. There was a tenth and eleventh "John" involved in the Monitor. Troy's General John Wool was commanding Fort Monroe at Hampton Roads. Finally, the captain of the Monitor itself, John L. Worden, gallantly directed the battle between his little 'cheese-box on a raft' and the Virginia (Merrimac) on that fateful and historic day on March 9, 1862.

Troy Chronicles

TROY'S "MONITOR BOYS"

DID YOU KNOW?

1. ENGINEER GEORGE GEER FROM TROY WROTE MORE THAN 80 LETTERS TO HIS WIFE ABOARD THE MONITOR.

2. GENERAL JOHN WOOL AT FORTRESS MONROE ALSO SERVED IN THE WAR OF 1812 AND THE MEXICAN-AMERICAN WAR. HE WAS COURT-MARSHALED FOR SIDING WITH THE NATIVES DURING THE INDIAN WARS BUT WAS NOT CONVICTED.

3. ENGINEER ROBINSON HANDS IS BURIED IN THE MT. IDA CEMETERY BUT HIS REMAINS MAY NOT BE THERE.

You learned that the turning point of the Civil War - the famous battle between the North's ironclad Monitor and South's Virginia (Merrimac) - had the "Made in Troy, NY" stamp all over it. But, as Paul Harvey often said, *"Now for the rest of the story."*

Troy's General John Wool, John Griswold (Wool's nephew) and John Winslow are often referred to in the history books, but you learned the names of the six Trojans who actually rolled the protective iron shields that beat back the guns of the Virginia. You will now learn the names of three more Trojans who actually took part in the battle aboard the Monitor on that historic day of March 9th, 1862!

George Spencer Geer was born in Troy around 1836 and married his sweetheart Martha Clark Hamilton on October 3, 1858 in New York City. On February 18, 1862, the blue eyed, brown hair Geer, standing at 5 feet 7 1/2 inches, enlisted as a first-class fireman in the Navy at New York City for a three-year term. By March 1862, he was assigned to the USS Monitor, where he served as the fireman until the ship sank in a storm on December 31, 1862. He survived and went on to be assigned as third assistant engineer on January 19, 1863, to the USS Galena (parts of which were also made in Troy). Geer went on to other ships and was honorably discharged on December 1, 1865. He worked on commercial steamers after that and while on a business trip on October 9, 1892, in Charleston, S.C, he died at the age of 56. He was sent home to Troy and buried in Oakwood Cemetery. George's wife continued to live at 171 Congress Street. She never remarried and died at the age of 85 on January 30, 1924.

William Henry Ives lived at 60 River Street in 1859. He worked as a fireman at the age of 12, on the Steamer John Mason running between Troy and Albany. However, he was working as an engineer for the Albany Iron Works when John Griswold promised him he could go to battle as the Monitor's engineer. It was Ives who directed the "energy of its powerful boilers" during the fight with the Virginia. After the war, he became rich in the invention of felt for steam pipes but lost

The Battle! J. Davidson painting.

his fortune and spent the rest of his life farming. He is buried in New Mount Ida Cemetery. His name has not been found on the official roster books so the Ives story may be false.

Robinson Woolen Hands was the 3rd Assistant Engineer on board the Monitor during its historic fight. However, very little is known of him. Some records indicate he was the second assistant engineer (Mark T. Sunstrom was also listed as 3rd assistant engineer). Hands was one of the four officers who went down with the Monitor when it sank on New Year's Eve off the coast of Cape Hatteras, North Carolina. There is a grave marker in his honor at the New Mount. Ida Cemetery.

In the annual report of the Secretary of the Navy for 1862, the following was written about the epic battle between the Monitor and Virginia (Merrimac):

Officers of the U.S. Monitor. Sitting on left is Robinson Hands, 3rd asst. engineer from Troy.

Troy Chronicles

"The fierce conflict between these two ironclads lasted for several hours. It was in appearance an unequal conflict, for the Merrimac was a large and noble structure, and the Monitor was in comparison almost diminutive. But the Monitor was strong in her armor, in the ingenious novelty of her construction, in the large caliber of her two guns, and the valor and skill with which she was handled. After several hours' fighting the Merrimac found herself overmatched, and, leaving the Monitor, sought to renew the attack on the Minnesota; but the Monitor again placed herself between the two vessels and reopened her fire upon her adversary. At noon the Merrimac, seriously damaged, abandoned the contest and, with her companions, retreated toward Norfolk.

Thus terminated the most remarkable naval combat of modern times, perhaps of any age. The fiercest and most formidable naval assault upon the power of the Union which has ever been made by the insurgents was heroically repelled, and a new era was opened in the history of maritime warfare."

The government recovered the Monitor turret and built a museum to house it. The two Troy foundries that made it, the Albany and Rennselaer Iron Works, now lay in ruins. The facade of the former is all that survives and the latter burned to the ground only a few years ago neglected by the city which owned it. Is that a fitting legacy?

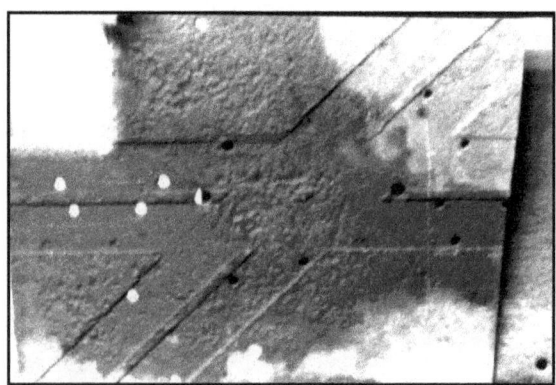

Extra hull plate rolled in Troy now at the Burden Museum.

Troy Chronicles

Chapter Three
ART

FAMOUS HISTORIC PAINTING OF TROY HAS WRONG TROY LOCATION

DID YOU KNOW?

1. THIS MAY BE ONE OF THE EARLIEST PORTRAITS OF THE CITY. TROY WAS INCORPORATED IN 1816.

2. THE PAINTING SAYS IT IS A VIEW FROM MT. IDA BUT IT IS ACTUALLY A VIEW FROM MT. OLYMPUS FROM A DIFFERENT PART OF THE CITY.

3. WILLIAM WALL IS CONSIDERED A FORERUNNER OF THE HUDSON RIVER SCHOOL.

During the late 18th and early 19th centuries many visitors from America and Europe and elsewhere visited the Hudson Valley and either wrote about their journey or painted various locations.

One such painter was William Guy Wall (1792 - 1864) an American painter of Irish descent. He was born in Dublin in 1792 and arrived in New York in 1812.

Wall became famous for his watercolor portrayals of the Hudson River Valley. A few of these watercolors were engraved by London born John Hill and his son John William

Troy Chronicles

Hill in a publication called the Hudson River Portfolio in 1820 and published by Henry Megary.

This was one of the first publications to make Americans stand and notice the beautiful American countryside. Wall is considered a forerunner of the Hudson River School. While in America (1812 to 1835; 1856-60) he was a founding member of the National Academy of Design (New York) and exhibited his works at such institutions as the Pennsylvania Academy of the Fine Arts (Philadelphia) and the Apollo Association (New York). He died in his hometown of Dublin in 1864.

Twenty of Wall's paintings were published in the Hudson River Portfolio in 1820. Megary in New York published them as aquatints in the early 1820s while Hill was the principal engraver. These images were some of the earliest images of the Hudson River and became quite popular with the public. Aquatint is intaglio printmaking and is a variety of the etching technique. It is not to be confused with Aquatint, a popular

Wall's view of Troy. Wrong title.

Troy Chronicles

Same vantage point but different artist. John Barber painted this in 1841 and it too is incorrect. It says Northern View of Troy, N.Y. from Mount Olympus. Technically it is the "Southern" view. Notice it is similar to Wall's. Text under the pictures says: "Mt. Olympus, from which the view was taken, is an elevation 120 feet in height, a short distance north of the city. The bridge across the Hudson, 1600 feet in length, with part of the flourishing village of West Troy, are seen on the right." Source: Internet

software program for the Mac that allows users to make glossy liquid images. Intaglio printmaking makes marks on a copper or zinc plate that can hold ink. The inked plate is then passed through a printing press together with a sheet of paper, resulting in a transfer of the inked image to the paper.

The effect makes the print look like a watercolor or wash drawing. Few people knew the process of Aquatint in the United States and Hill became the best-known user of the technique. In 1819 twenty plates that he did were published in Picturesque Views of American Scenery (1820-21) in four volumes, the first major plate book published in the US.

Troy Chronicles

Photograph taken from Mount Olympus prior to 1862 (wooden Green Island Bridge can be seen in the pix – burned in 1862). This is a similar view and probably the same spot where Barber and Wall painted their views. Source: Don Rittner.

Shortly after the completion of in Picturesque Views of American Scenery he was commissioned by New York printer Megary to engrave and color views of William G. Wall's New York scenes. The resulting Hudson River Portfolio (1821-1825) contained twenty views of New York State towns, cities, and landscapes.

Here is the problem. One of Wall's later paintings is titled "Troy From Mount Ida" (#11 in one of the Portfolio publications) and shows a tranquil view of the early city (Troy was chartered as a city in 1816) from an elevated view looking south. The view shows a couple of people walking along a dirt road on their way to the city which is seen nestled on the

Troy Chronicles

W. H. Bartlett's View of Troy from Mount Ida in 1939 is the correct Mt. Ida view. You can see Albany in the distance.

eastern meander of the Hudson River, with Helderbergs in the background and a few islands (Starbuck or Center Island, Adams Island and Storm Island) in the river.

The only problem with the print is the label. It is NOT a view from Mt. Ida, but rather a view from Mt. Olympus, a smaller rock outcrop (100+ feet high) located in the north central part of the city situated between Rennselaer Street on the south and North Street on the north, Currently 5th Avenue runs through it (I believe in the 1950s it was cut through). Mt. Olympus at one time had an octagonal "summer house" (tavern) on its peak in 1823, and owned by W.D. Vanderheyden. He served on warm nights, *"cooling cordials and other beverages"* to visitors. It burned on Feb. 13, 1830, a Sunday night.

By examining the painting you see the elevation is not that great and the river is nearby not far from the "river" road. What is amazing is that this original road is not the present

Troy Chronicles

Original River Road as seen in Wall's painting. Now called North First Street. Photo by Don Rittner.

River Street but North First Street, now considered an alley. North First Street is a cobblestone street and originally began at the original Vanderheyden Ferry at Ferry Street and went to Schaghticoke. It is remarkable that Troy's first road is still partially intact.

It seems obvious to me that Wall knew it was Mt. Olympus and not Mt. Ida (present Prospect Park). The two views are totally different. On Mt. Olympus, looking south would give you the view of the emerging new city, as depicted in the painting. That same view from Mt. Ida would show a more barren landscape as South Troy was not laid out until the 1840s or so. And in fact there is a painting from Mt. Ida done in 1872 by Bartlett that shows South Troy (pretty desolate) and Albany and the Helderbergs in the distance.

So the question is, who made the mistake? Probably the printer Megary or engraver Hill but who gave them the erroneous title? Maybe on the other hand, Hall after having a few drinks from Vanderheyden's summer house later could not remember if he was on Mt. Olympus or Ida and just tossed a coin with the title. We will never know I suppose but at last the mystery of the erroneous title has been solved.

Troy Chronicles

RARE DRAWING OF TROY FINALLY IDENTIFIED

Did You Know?

1. This is one of the earliest drawings of Troy now identified.

2. John Hill worked for the New York State Geological Survey as the draftsman for the Zoological Department under James Ellsworth De Kay.

3. This same view can be seen today while standing on a balcony in an apartment complex that now sits on what was farmland in the painting.

I like discovering things. While I was doing research on the misidentified painting of Troy by William Wall, I noticed that the NY Historical Society had in its folder a drawing they thought might have been of Troy but was uncertain. So, I offered to look at it and see if I could assist. Here are my findings.

From my research I have concluded that this drawing depicts the City of Troy, NY from the period 1793-1835.

The question is did John Hill or John William Hill do this drawing? I can attribute this to John William Hill (1812-1879). He lived in Nyack, N.Y. by 1836, moving there after working for his father, the well-known engraver John Hill, for fourteen years in NYC. We know that in his 20s the younger Hill worked for the New York State Geological Survey (the NYSGS began in 1836). He was the draftsman for the

Troy Chronicles

Zoological Department under James Ellsworth De Kay (also beginning in 1836) and did the illustrations for a 5-volume work under that department in 1842-43. The NYSGS was located in nearby Albany. He created topographic and overhead views of cities and towns and this drawing fits perfectly in that genre and also time frame. Between 1830 and 1832, the younger Hill drew a series of five Erie Canal views that his father engraved. This would have brought the younger Hill to Troy during that time and that fits in well with my dating of this view.

The elder Hill worked on Wall's Hudson River Portfolio (1821-25) and may have inspired to do his own views including this one of Troy. There is a Wall painting of Troy that Hill engraved though misnamed View From Mt. Ida (was in fact Mt. Olympus). If the elder Hill was responsible for engraving the wrong description it would tell me he was not familiar with the Troy area and likely not the artist of this drawing in question.

I think considering the detail given to the landscape (geology) and time frame, this is more likely to have been done by John William Hill during the time he was drawing the Erie Canal views between 1830-1832.

The findings are based on an examination of the drawing and the location of well-known Troy landmarks of the time, their spatial relationship to each other, and the landforms in general. The view is drawn from Latham, N.Y. just above West Troy (now Watervliet). Troy can be seen on the east shore of the Hudson River while West Troy can be seen on the west side of the river. The topography from the vantage point of the illustrator is in the area off Route 2 in the Eastview Drive area of present Watervliet.

There are several known landmarks in this drawing of Troy that can be identified. They are numbered on the map and explained below.

Troy Chronicles

The numbered items were identified and helped date this rare Troy drawing.

Number 1

This is the George Tibbits Mansion built about 1797 (George and his brother moved to Troy from Lansingburgh in 1797). Kathy Sheehan from the Rensselaer County Historical Society

tells me the mansion is on the 1818 Klein map of Troy, the earliest map of the city and falls within this date range. We know that on the left (north) of this mansion in 1879 was built the Gale Chapel and School. So we know the etching is not that old since Gale is not shown on the drawing.

Number 2

This is Congress Street heading up the hill going east and the Tibbits Mansion was located on the NE corner of 7th Ave and Congress. This fits in well with the rest of the spatial locations of known landmarks in Troy at the time and is adjacent to the Tibbits Mansion in the right location.

Number 3

This is the most telling of all in this artwork. This shows the iconic four spire St Paul's Episcopal Church on the NE

corner of Third and State Street. It was built in 1826-1828. This church has some interesting history and can be found on one of my articles at:

http://blog.timesunion.com/rittner/twas-the-night-before-christmas-began-in-troy/1242/

Number 4

This goes with Number 3 spatially. It is the First Baptist Church also on Third Street, not far, just south of St. Paul's. Both of the steeples on this church and St Paul's match on the drawing. The present church was built in 1816. The earlier one had a square tower and plain steeple (as shown). The arrow wind vane currently on the church steeple is the same as in the drawing.

Number 5

This is the steeple of the First Presbyterian Church on the NE Corner of First and Congress Streets, two blocks west of the Baptist church and one block south. First Presbyterian

Troy Chronicles

Church. NE Corner of Congress and First. (now Seminary Park).

We know this church was built in 1793 and taken down in 1836.

Number 6

Troy was built on a flood plain of the Hudson River which you can see (#6) and to the east is the Taconic Plateau, very well depicted here.

Number 7

This represents Washington Square, now called Monument Square. The angle of these buildings is in the right configuration on the map.

Troy Chronicles

Also here you can see the Hudson River and the village of West Troy on the west side of the river. You can see the small grouping of buildings to the right of the illustration. West Troy was settled around 1823 (now city of Watervliet, combined with Gibbonsville and Port Schuyler) in 1896.

Numbers 8 & 9

These two illustrations of wagons and workers are very telling. First the farmer on the right (#9) is holding a typically Dutch designed hay-rake and pitchfork. These are classic 17th-18th century Dutch designs. The wagon (#8) called a Conestoga wagon is usually attributed to German innovation in the Conestoga area of Pennsylvania. However, the truth is that this style of wagon is very Dutch AND German. If you look at many of the 17th Dutch Masters paintings you will see variations of these type of wagons. These are Dutch symbols and probably represent a time when Troy was earlier called Vanderheyden after the Dutch family that settled there, until 1789 when the citizens changed it to Troy. The insertion of these Dutch farmers could indicate that Hill was just

paying homage to the Dutch roots of Troy or it could represent the fact that there were still many Dutch farmers in and around Troy during this time. My dating of these drawing is around 1793-1831 so is well within the memory of the Dutch founding of the city, but still had many Dutch inhabitants in the region.

Number 10

Poestenkill Valley (Mount Ida) is the site of some of Troy's earliest industries and is just off (south) of Congress Street. The valley and its orientation is depicted correctly in this drawing.

Chapter Four
CULTURE

HOLLYWOOD ON THE HUDSON

DID YOU KNOW?

1. MAUREEN STAPLETON WAS BORN IN 1925 AND GREW UP ON FIRST STREET IN TROY.

2. DRAMA WAS PERFORMED ABOVE THE MARKET HOUSE IN THE 19TH CENTURY WHICH HOUSED BUTCHERS AND FARMERS ON THE FIRST FLOOR.

3. TV AND MOVIE ACTOR ROBERT FULLER WAS BORN IN TROY.

Troy has a long history of entertainment going back to the days before the city was even incorporated. Entertainment however comes in many forms.

On May 20th, 1793, at Ashley's Tavern on Ferry Street, a Mr. Moore, entertained with a series of lectures - apparently a set of humorous remarks - for an admission of 2 shillings and six pence for adults. (kids cost one shilling and six pence). A few years later, in October 1800, an African Lion was exhibited for a few days. On October 8, 1805 a live elephant was exhibited at Moulton's Coffee House (where Russell Sage is now) also for a short period. These were considered exotic animals of course and would have created quite an interest.

Musical contributions were recorded as early as 1822 at Babcock's Hotel on River Street. Somewhere in between an

Troy Chronicles

exhibit of a dwarf cow and an educated bear which could read, spell, subtract, multiply and divide, was music on King David's Cymbal, an ancient instrument, and music on the Leaf, accompanied by violin and organ. A year later, a Mr. Keene gave a vocal concert along with the piano.

On Fifth Avenue and Ferry Street at Mr. Churchill's Storeroom, you could hear the theatrical performance of Mr. and Mrs. Russell and daughter. Their performances of moral plays were only 25 cents admission. Front seats were for ladies only.

As early as 1829, Troy's Public Markets offered drama. Get your meat on the first floor and entertainment on the second. The second floor of the North Market on Federal Street was opened on July 4 with a play called 'Pizarro, or the Death of Rollo.' In Feb, 1847, the hall on the second floor of Fulton Market, at the corner of Fulton and River Streets opened with the play, 'The Lady of Lyons.' Across the street at the Peale Troy Museum, 'Uncle Sam's Cabin' was first performed in the U.S. in 1882.

Troy had several burlesque and vaudeville houses as it moved into the 20th century and of course several movie houses when the talkies became popular. Troy was no stranger to producing original music either in the vein of grand marches, waltzes, or ragtime. During the Ragtime era, a daughter was born to a woman who worked for the Labor Department. This baby would grow up a woman who would become a star of the stage, screen, and later television.

Local folks like to point out that the Capital District area was the home of several stars of the stage and screen during the golden years. Kirk Douglas, and Bill Devane are often tossed out. But here in Troy, we have two ladies that the city is famous for: Helen of Troy, more mythical; and Maureen Stapleton, a living legend.

Troy Chronicles

Troy's Maureen Stapleton above in "Reds" and below with the author at her residence a few years before her death.

Maureen Stapleton is all Troy! Born in 1925, she grew up on First Street in Troy. Maureen is one of the few actresses that have crossed over to all media and was successful in film, theater, and TV.

Her first major stage success was in The Rose Tattoo (1951). She is best known for intelligent character roles. Her first appearance on Broadway was in Orpheus Descending (1957), Toys in the Attic (1960), The Gingerbread Lady (1970), and The

Troy Chronicles

Country Girl (1973). Her films include A View from the Bridge (1962), Plaza Suite (1972), Reds (1982), Cocoon (1985), and Nuts (1988). She even did the voice in Snow Cat, the 1998 animation. She won the Academy Award for supporting actress for her performance in Reds in 1981.

Her career spans some four decades and as one reviewer said *"she has received the highest acclaim for her great emotional power and versatility."*

She is a charter member of the renowned Actors Studio, and has won the top honors granted to performing artists, including the Oscar, Emmy and Tony Awards. Few actors have been so successful in all media.

In 1995, she and Jane Scoville wrote her autobiography called "A Hell Of A Life," full of great stories. Another book, "Maureen Stapleton: A Bio Bibliography" is the first book dedicated to the career of this consummate actress.

In 1981, her Academy Award year, Hudson Valley Community College dedicated the Maureen Stapleton Theater with the actress there to help celebrate the rededication of the Maureen Stapleton Theater. Hudson Valley Community College presented a film festival showcasing highlights of her film career.

For years before her death, I sent her crossword puzzle books every month. For some reason Trojan women love to do crossword puzzles.

Troy Chronicles

PLAY IT AGAIN, HELEN

Did You Know?

1. George Kaufman went on to win the Pulitzer Prize for Drama in 1932 and 1937.

2. Helen was Kaufman's second play.

3. Troy's Cluett & Peabody Company contracted with artist Joseph C. Leyendecker to develop a winning look for their Arrow collars. The result was the first successful introduction of sex as a selling tool. Helen of Troy, NY was a spoof of that.

Ah, the roaring twenties. It's a decade I wish I experienced. However, the year 1923 was particularly interesting. It's the year that the first wireless telephone call was made from New York to London. Jack Dempsey defended his heavyweight boxing title against Luis Firpo. Yankee Stadium opened in New York City and Rin Tin Tin made his film debut.

Oh yeah, more plays were produced on Broadway in the 20s than in any other period, and in 1923, the city of Troy was featured in a hit musical called Helen of Troy, New York.

Helen was written by the legendary George S. Kaufman (1889-1961) and Marc Connelly (1890-1980), from their book of the same name. The musical numbers were written by Bert Kalmar and Harry Ruby with titles like: Look For The Happy Ending ; It Was Meant To Be; Cry Baby; Keep A Goin' (the show's hit song); The Small Town Girl; I Like A Big Town, I Like A Small Town; What Makes a Business Man Tired; What

Troy Chronicles

Helen Ford was born in Troy and played the lead in Helen of Troy, N.Y.

The Girls Will Wear; My Ideal; Nijigo Novgo; and Helen Of Troy, New York.

Kaufman, a playwright and journalist, was the most successful writer in American Theater between World War I and II. He won the Pulitzer Prize twice for plays of which he was coauthor. He wrote some 40 plays and half were hits. He was the drama critic for The New York Times from 1917 to 1930.

His first successful play Dulcy, starring Lynn Fontanne, was written in collaboration with Marc Connelly and first performed in 1921. Two years later, they wrote the two-act Helen of Troy, New York, starring Helen Ford.

Connelly was also a playwright and journalist for the Morning Telegraph covering the theater. He's famous for his Pulitzer Prize winning Green Pastures, a story of the old testament through the lives of southern blacks, but especially is known for his comedies that he co-wrote with Kaufman.

Kaufman and Connelly's Dulcy was followed by To the Ladies (1922) with Helen Hayes, and then Helen of Troy, New York.

The musical Helen of Troy, New York opened on Broadway on Tuesday, June 19, 1923, at the Selwyn Theater on 42nd

Troy Chronicles

Street at 8:30. The play was introduced by Rufus LeMaire and George Jessel. I can only imagine the opening remarks by Jessel - "Take my collar, please."

Though some reviewers were not crazy about the score (one did call it "competent and catchy music"), Kaufman and Connelly received raves.

Helen of Troy, New York was based on the story of working girls in the collar industry of Troy and pokes fun at the new corporate culture that was taking hold in America. This was modeled from the very successful advertising campaign of Cluett, Peabody that ran from 1905 to 1931. The collar company's ad campaign appeared nationally and in particular in the Saturday Evening Post, an upscale magazine.

The Cluett company contracted with artist Joseph C. Leyendecker to develop a winning look for their Arrow collars. The result was the first successful introduction of sex as a selling tool; all of his beautifully illustrated ads showed male and female models responding to the sex appeal of the 'Arrow Man.' During this time, most men in the country were wearing collars from Troy, but made from a number of collar companies. Cluett cashed in by creating the 'Arrow Man' and captured most of the market. This was the predecessor of the now familiar 'Marlboro Man' and other brand "models" that followed. Helen of Troy, New York seems to be a response to this, and besides lampooning mass advertising, the play was rather eccentric and even had a weird number with Russian folk dancers and an instrumental number with ukuleles and other strange instruments.

Troy Chronicles

One writer wasn't surprised at the eccentricity considering that Kaufman eventually wrote three Marx Brothers movies (The Cocoanuts (1929); Animal Crackers (1930); A Night at the Opera (1935), while his buddies Kalmar and Ruby wrote the songs for Animal Crackers. Kalmar and Ruby also wrote Horse Feathers (1932) and Duck Soup (1933) in addition to the music.

Regardless, I believe I have tracked down the play and much of the score and plan on bringing the play back to life in Troy. So, if you can act, send me email. Who knows, you could become the next Helen of Troy, and that's no duck soup.

Here is one of the songs from the play - Keep it Going: http://www.collectionscanada.gc.ca/obj/028011/f3/11570.ram

Troy Chronicles

HOLLYWOOD VIA TROY
PART ONE

DID YOU KNOW?

1. CARLYLE BLACKWELL SR. (JANUARY 20, 1884-JUNE 17, 1955) IS THE OLDEST TROJAN ENTRY TO HOLLYWOOD STARTING WITH THE 1909 VITAGRAPH. HE APPEARED IN 89 MOVIES, SPANNING 40 YEARS FROM 1910 TO 1947.

2. HELEN FORD (JUNE 6, 1894-JANUARY 19, 1982) WHO PLAYED THE LEAD IN THE KAUFMAN PLAY "HELEN OF TROY, NEW YORK." WAS
ACTUALLY BORN HERE TOO.

3. THE NASH SISTERS (MARY & FLORENCE) REAL LAST NAME IS RYAN.

We know that Maureen Stapleton, star of stage, screen and theater was born on First Street. We also know Troy is currently a popular backdrop for Hollywood productions. Did you know Troy has been involved in Hollywood for more than 100 years?

Some two dozen actors, actresses, directors, producers, or writers have been born here. Let's start from the beginning.

Troy Chronicles

The 19th Century

Marie L. Day. b. 1855 - November 7, 1939.

Day acted during the 1920's-30's appearing in three movies: Timothy's Quest (1922), The Ragged Edge (1923) and Mother Carey's Chickens (1938).

Mike Ready. August 21, 1858 - March 26, 1936.

Ready was another early actor appearing in but two films: Rough Ridin' (1924) and Warming Up (1928), in which he played himself.

Frank Terry. May 3, 1870 - October 26, 1948.

Born Frank Ernest Edwards, Terry originally toured the European and Asian stage as "Nat Clifford." He returned to America as a gagman for silent film comedies. On August 24th, 1919, while on set, he handed what was thought a dummy bomb to "Harold Lloyd." It exploded in Lloyd's hands losing two fingers and a thumb from his right hand. Terry became "Laurel and Hardy's" comedy film writer in the 1920's-30's, and also acted as a bit player. He acted in 9 movies, including playing a hunter in the 1935 classic Bride of Frankenstein. He left Hollywood becoming a missionary chaplain to a leper colony in Hawaii.

William Worthington , April 8, 1872-April 9, 1941

Worthington's career was versatile, spanning 40 years, from 1913 to 1942, acting in 85 films He also directed some 37 movies from 1915-25, and produced the 1917 movie The Clock. He appeared in classics such as the 1933 Marx Brother's Duck Soup (First Minister of Finance), 1934 Perils of Pauline (the American Consul), and 1938 Boys Town (the Governor).

Troy Chronicles

Joe Brandt, July 20, 1882-February 22, 1939.

Brandt was a writer and penned the scenario in the 1915 movie Graft.

Carlyle Blackwell Sr., January 20, 1884-June 17, 1955.

Carlye is the oldest Trojan entry to Hollywood starting with the 1909 Vitagraph. He appeared in 89 movies, spanning 40 years from 1910 to 1947. His first performance was Uncle Tom's Cabin (1910), incidentally first performed on stage in America in Troy 48 years earlier. Other notable films include The Badge of Courage (1912). Blackwell was also a director, producer, and writer. He is the father of actor Carlyle Blackwell.

Mary Nash. August 15, 1885-December 3, 1976.

Born Mary Ryan, Nash appeared in 25 films in the 1910's to 40's. She played Mrs. Pryor in Wells Fargo (1937), Frulein Rottenmeier in Heidi (1937), and Margaret Lord in The Philadelphia Story (1940).

Albert Herman. February 22, 1887-September 28, 1958.

Herman did it all. He was a director, producer, production manager and designer, in the art department, and writer from 1920's to 40's. As director, he's credited with 59 movies including many westerns. His last film Rogues' Gallery (1945), he also produced, as well as six other movies from 1931-45. He was the production manager for four movies, production designer for two, was art associate for Mr. Doodle Kicks Off (1938), and writer of The Black Coin (1936).

Florence Nash. October 2, 1888-April 2, 1950.

Florence Ryan was the sister of Mary Nash and so became Florence Nash. However, her acting career only produced

Troy Chronicles

three movies Springtime (1914), It's a Great Life (1936) and The Women (1939), proving sequels, in any form, never really do make it.

Edward Butcher. May 15, 1892-December 11, 1960.

Butcher was a producer in Hollywood with seven pictures to his credit from 1930 to 35.

Helen Ford. June 6, 1894-January 19, 1982.

The real "Helen of Troy, New York," Ford appeared in 8 movies from the 1940's to 70's, but had an earlier career on the stage. She appeared in the lead in George F. Kaufman's 'Helen of Troy, New York' a Broadway play in 1923 based around the Troy collar industry.

Jack Boland. January 23, 1896-.

Boland was famous as a second unit or assistant director on more than a dozen films from 1924 to 1958, including the 1958 Littlest Hobo.

Lester Cole. March 30 1896 -May 4, 1962.

Cole appeared in only four films from 1929-44: The Desert Song, Painted Faces (1929), Love at First Sight (1930) and South of Dixie (1944).

Alan Birmingham. (no dates)

Birmingham appeared in 7 movies from 1929-37, including roles such as Dr. Cummings in The Furies (1930) and the role of Lamb in The Great Gambini (1937).

Troy Chronicles

HOLLYWOOD VIA TROY
PART TWO

DID YOU KNOW?

1. TROY'S TOM LEWIS, HUSBAND OF LORETTA YOUNG, STARTED THE ARMED FORCES RADIO SERVICE.

2. ROBERT FULLER IS REMEMBERED FOR HIS ROLES AS JESS HARPER IN THE TV SERIES LARAMIE (1959).

3. ROBERT ALLEN WROTE "IT'S NOT FOR ME TO SAY" FOR THE MOVIE LIZZIE IN 1957. JOHNNY MATHIS BROUGHT IT NUMBER 5 ON BILLBOARD. BING CROSBY ALSO RECORDED A VERSION.

In a previous column we talked about Troy-born actors of the 19th century that made a mark on Hollywood. This week we will demonstrate that Trojan-born contributions to Hollywood continue right up to the present. This list will surprise some baby boomers as well as the younger set.

The Golden Years

Tom Lewis. July 8, 1901-May 20, 1988.

Tom Lewis, born in Lansingburgh, was a producer and writer doing both on Cause for Alarm! (1951) and producing a TV episode of The Indiscreet Mrs. Jarvis (1955). He was married to Loretta Young and produced two years of her TV hit, The Loretta Young Show.

Troy Chronicles

Maureen Stapleton. June 21, 1925- March 13, 2006

More than 52 movies, a dozen TV appearances, and award winning stage performances, puts Trojan Maureen Stapleton in a class of her own. Born on First Street, she is one of few actors to win all three major acting awards: Oscar, Tony, and Emmy. She loved to do crossword puzzles and play charades and the author had the privilege to play with her.

Philip O'Brien. May 23, 1927 - January 9, 1999.

O'Brien was on the short list to become Obi-Wan Kenobi in Star Wars. His career began late in life spanning the 80's and 90's. He appeared in 18 movies and TV appearances. He was the American coach in Chariots of Fire (1981), the Maitre d' in Batman (1989), and Earl in Who Framed Roger Rabbit (1988). His TV appearances include The Ted Kennedy Jr. Story(1986), Love with the Perfect Stranger (1988) and Goldeneye: The Secret Life of Ian Fleming (1989).

Robert Allen. February 5, 1928 - October 1, 2000.

Allen was a composer, conductor, arranger, pianist and accompanist for Peter Lind Hayes, as well as actor from the 30's to 50's. He composed songs and scores for TV series such as "Studio One" (1948) and "Playhouse 90" (1956), and the song "It's Not for Me to Say" for the movie Lizzie (1957). He played himself in the 1938 and 1941, Hal Kemp and His Orchestra movies.

Bob Turley. September 19, 1930 – March 30, 2013.

Robert Lee Turley played himself in the movie New York Yankees (The Movie) (1987). 'Bullet Bob' wasn't really an actor but a baseball pitcher for the SL Browns, Baltimore Orioles [All-Star: 1954], NY Yankees [World Series: 1955 1958, 1960; All-Star: 1955, 1958; Cy Young Award: 1958], Boston Red Sox, and Los Angeles Angels.

Troy Chronicles

Robert Fuller. July 29, 1934.

You know Robert from TV and movies spanning a career from the 1950's to 90's. He began with a bit part and acting lessons from Richard Boone (Have Gun, Will Travel) in Marilyn Monroe's Gentlemen Prefer Blondes (1953). Fuller is remembered for his roles as Jess Harper in the TV series Laramie (1959) and Cooper Smith in Wagon Train (1957), or Dr. Kelly Brackett in Emergency! (1972). He was also in the movies Return of the Seven (1966) and Maverick (1994). His TV appearances include Walker, Texas Ranger, as recently as last May, and Seinfeld, Kung Fu: The Legend Continues, Diagnosis Murder, and about 40 others.

Tom Vaughn. February 28, 1943.

Ok, not really an actor, he played defensive tackle for the National Football League's Detroit Lions (1965-1971), but he did appear in the movie Paper Lion (1968), playing himself.

And The Tradition Continues...

James Gorman. March 8, 1961.

Forty-year-old James Gorman has produced 5 movies including the 1998 Les Miserable and S.O.S. (2001), and wrote and produced Cutthroat Island (1995).

Russell Wong. March 1, 1963.

Russell Wong is a former dancer and photographer. Today, he is a familiar face and perhaps the most successful of the new crop of Trojan-born actors. He has appeared in 23 movies already including New Jack City (1991), The Joy Luck Club (1993) and has made appearances in TV shows such as Vanishing Son, 21 Jump Street, and Touched by an Angel. His brother is actor Michael Wong who is married to model Janet Ma.

Troy Chronicles

Kevin Gardner. December 1, 1969.

I was enjoying the then present memories of Woodstock (the real one) and the first man landing on the moon the year Kevin Gardner was born! Since then, Kevin has appeared in the TV movie Confessions of a Sorority Girl (1993) and made numerous appearances on the TV show Saved by the Bell: The New Class (1993).

Next?

Besides actors, Troy has become a set for several movies: The Bostonians, (1984); Ironweed (1987); The Age of Innocence, (1993); Scent of a Women (1992); The Opponent, (2000), and filmed, but not released yet is The Palace Thief (2002) and The Time Machine (2002). I had a bit part in Ironweed and Age of Innocence, but for some reason Hollywood isn't calling?

Troy Chronicles

'TWAS THE NIGHT BEFORE CHRISTMAS

DID YOU KNOW?

1. THIS POEM FIRST APPEARED IN PRINT ON DECEMBER 23, 1823 IN THE TROY SENTINEL NEWSPAPER.

2. THE POEM WAS GIVEN TO THE EDITOR BY HARRIET BUTLER, DAUGHTER OF THE PASTOR OF ST. PAUL'S CHURCH AND FRIEND OF CLEMENT MOORE.

3. IT IS ONE OF THE MOST PARODIED POEMS OF ALL TIME, AS EVIDENCED HERE.

Twas the night before Christmas, and all through this land
I could not find a worker, who would understand.
I wanted to buy presents for my three little boys,
But the mall rats were just talking and making such noise!

The workers were nestled all dressed in their shreds,
While visions of closing time danced in their heads.
I stood there all snow bound and wanting some help,
"I want to spend money," I pleaded and yelped.

I entered each store but it didn't really matter,
As each mall clerk saw me, they hurried and scattered.
A bundle of nerves, I laid on my back,
To lower my stress, and to keep focused - on track.

When out of the mall, I heard such a clatter,
"Buy on the Net, and keep your wallet fatter."
So away to my Mac, I flew like a flash,
Logged on to eBay, and shelled out my cash.

Troy Chronicles

But the moon on the breast of the new-fallen snow,
Gave light to my purchases, the quality was low.
I tossed up my hands, giving up I feared,
But then a small sleigh and eight reindeer appeared.

19th Century Cartoonist Thomas Nast gave us the look of Santa Claus.

Troy Chronicles

With a little old driver, so lively and quick,
I knew in a minute, he wasn't some hick,
But our dear Uncle Sam to lay down the claim,
"Buy it in Troy," and uttered the names:

Buy Clements! Buy Book Outlet! Buy Illium Cafe too!
A stroll down River Street for antiques or brand new!
To the top of your wish list, be it large or small,
Spend your cash, spend your cash, spend it here - all!

Like toadstools springing from a fresh morning rain,
The shoppers, and me, spread through our city of fame,
And up to the cash registers, these shoppers all flew,
Spending in Troy like Sam wanted us to!

And then, with an inkling, we gave him the proof,
Spending in Troy wasn't a goof!,
As I opened my wallet, and lay the cash down,
Another good shopper appeared with a bound.

This new found Trojan from his foot to his head,
Knew that Troy's greatness would again spread and spread.
A bundle of deeds he held in his hand,
From buying as much Troy as he possibly can.

His eyes -- still they twinkled! His vision how merry!
He shouted with glee at the bargains he carried.
No matter the cold, or the air that was misty,
He loved buying buildings holding Troy's great history.

No more buildings boarded atop or beneath,
He flatly declared and gritted his teeth,
We will fix all the streets and even the alleys,
Then get all Trojans to wake up and rally!

Troy Chronicles

He was certain and sure but I still had some fear,
That our great buildings would soon go, no more shopping sprees here.
But a wink of his eye and a twist of his head,
Soon gave me to know I had nothing to dread.

And then I remembered and started to cheer,
A new group of citizens will rule this New Year.
I stepped back, regrouped, I knew of our task,
Spreading the word that our future's still our past.

I walked with all smiles down River and whistled,
My worries away, they flew like the down of a thistle.
Not far in the future, Troy again will stand tall,
So, HAPPY HOLIDAYS! From one Trojan to all!

Troy Sentinel building where Moore's poem was first published in 1823. Photo by Don Rittner.

Troy Chronicles

WILL THE REAL HELEN STAND UP!

Did You Know?

1. A 10-foot mural of Helen of Troy painted by well-known area muralist David Lithgow depicts Helen flanked on both sides by a Troy female collar worker and a male foundry man. It was buried behind a false wall for more than 50 years.

2. In 1904 Wilfrid S. Jackson penned the 307-page humorous romance novel, "Helen of Troy, N.Y."

3. Comedian George Jessel produced the Kaufman play Helen of Troy, N.Y.

"There's no Greece, just natural good grooming." Helen of Troy, N.Y.

I found the above quote as part of an ad in a 1959 Cambridge, Mass newspaper showing the profile of a woman pushing Wildroot Cream-Oil for men. We all know about the mythical Trojan War version of Helen, but a little research has shown that our own Helen of Troy, N.Y. was a pretty popular subject in the roaring 20's and throughout the 20th century.

A couple of years ago, a previous owner of Proctor's Theater ripped out a false wall to reveal a 10-foot mural of our own Helen of Troy. The mural, painted by well-known area muralist David Lithgow depicts Helen flanked on both sides by a Troy female collar worker and a male foundry man. It no doubt impressed all that entered the Vaudeville theater when it opened in 1913.

Troy Chronicles

Perhaps this twist on the classic Helen began as early as 1904 when Wilfrid S. Jackson penned the 307-page humorous romance novel, "Helen of Troy, N.Y." Jackson and his wife Emilie, also a writer, are both well known for translating other works of fiction. However, Helen is an original story about a rich socialite and German American, Helen B. Heimer from Troy, N.Y. and those interested in marrying her.

A connection between Helen and Troy's Arrow collars developed early in the 20th century. Cole Porter sang about Arrow collars in his 1912 "A Football King (aka 'If I Were

Helen mural in the entry of Proctor's Theater Troy. Photo by Don Rittner.

Troy Chronicles

Only A Football Man'). The original title was intended for the initiation play "The Pot Of Gold" for Yale's Delta Kappa Epsilon, but it wasn't used so he revised it and sung it with the Yale Glee Club during his senior year (1912-13), when he served as the club's president:

For my autograph I'd charge a dollar,
And I'd be the title of an Arrow collar,
Such a very muddy sort of very bloody sort of thing.
My opponents I should give a scalding
That would make me rival Captain Jesse Spalding.
If they'd only realize that I'm a football King.

After World War I, returning soldiers demanded wearing shirts with soft attached collars, signaling the end of the more stiff detachable collars. The Arrow shirt with collar was invented by Troy's Cluett-Peabody & Sons to satisfy those needs.

In 1915, Frederick Peabody created a new advertising campaign to promote these shirts and hired the popular commercial artist, J.D. Leyendecker to come up with the famous Arrow collar man. The Arrow collar man became the symbol of the perfect American male. Leyendecker's ads, found in magazines in the US and Canada, were a big hit, and he found himself the male "pin up" along with many marriage proposals from women throughout the 1930s. Never mind the fact that Leyendecker was outwardly gay and his male models were often his lovers.

We next find Helen of Troy, N.Y. in the plot of one of the early Rouge detective stories. The overweight, slow, cigar smoking, ill-kept, detective Jim Hanvey, created by writer Octavus Roy Cohen (1891-1959) was one of America's earliest private eyes and appeared in short stories, mainly in the Saturday Evening Post. One episode entitled, Helen of Troy, N.Y. was published in the October 7, 1922 Post and in The Detective Magazine on January 5, 1923.

Troy Chronicles

It was the Arrow Collar Man that inspired George Kaufman and Marc Connelly to write the book and 2-act play of Helen of Troy, N.Y. The play appeared in New York City's Selwyn Theatre from June to October 1923, followed by a stint in the Times Square Theater from October 8, 1923 to December 1, for a total of 191 performances.

The 1923 play was a big hit and starred Helen Ford as Helen of Troy. Ironic, since Helen was actually born here in Troy on June 6, 1897 as Helen Isabel Barnett. This play also ran for three days at the premier opening of the Fairmont Theater in Fairmont, West Virginia on June 4, 1923.

George Jessel (yes, the comedian) produced the play and it launched the career of music writers Bert Kalmar and Harry Ruby.

They later went on to write for the Marx Brothers movies.

Another songwriter who penned a tune for the play was Lorenz Hart (of Rodgers & Hart fame) who with W. Frank Harling wrote "Moonlight Lane." This collaboration with Harling is one of the few published songs Hart wrote with a composer other than Richard Rodgers. You can hear this song performed on the CD Hollywood Party [Bayview RNBW009]. You can also download and listen to "Keep A-Going", one of the show's songs written by Byron Gay and recorded in Canada in 1924 by the Andy Tipaldi Orchestra (go to http://www.collectionscanada.gc.ca/obj/028011/f3/11570.ram).

Troy Chronicles

HELEN OF TROY, N.Y. - ACT II

DID YOU KNOW?

1. A SHORT STORY TITLED "MYTH AND MAGIC: HELEN OF TROY, NEW YORK" WAS WRITTEN BY PAULA DETMER RIGGS IN 1966.

2. A SHORT SILENT FILM "HELENE OF TROY, N.Y" STARRING AL COOKE CANNOT BE FOUND.

3. POET PETER VIERECK PENNED "TO HELEN OF TROY, N.Y." IN 1978.

"Helen of Troy, N.Y." was the larger-than-life mural at the inside entrance of Troy's Proctor's Theater, the center of a novel, a diamond-robbing moll of the Roaring Twenties, and the center of a Kaufman-Connelly Broadway play in 1923.

Shortly after the successful Broadway play, Harry Charles Witwer (1880-1929), a writer and screenwriter of the first half of the 20th century, apparently suggested a movie version of "Helen." An advertisement (lantern slide) I found for the movie was presented by the British-owned Film Booking Offices of America, Inc. (FBO) as "Helene of Troy, N.Y." not "Helen," and billed as "Another One of the Beauty Parlor Series Suggested by the Famous H.C. Witwer, Cosmopolitan Magazine Stories." It starred Al Cooke and Kit Guard and had a supporting cast of Lorraine Easton, Thelma Hill, and Danny O'Shea. It was directed by Arvid Gilstrom. The ad boasts "More Laughs Than an Ant Hill Has Ants!." I believe it was a silent movie, not a talkie.

Witwer wrote for many of the leading magazines of the day and also penned a number of screenplays himself. I could not find any article written about Helen by him, nor could I find anything about the movie other than the lantern slide, so how he "suggested" it is puzzling. Film Booking Offices released 444 films between 1926 and 1929 and "Helene of Troy, N.Y." is not listed anywhere.

This British movie distributor became the centerpiece of Joe Kennedy's (President Kennedy's father) entrance into Hollywood. Using insider information he received, Kennedy bought the FBO, and then used the profits from FBO to purchase the Radio Corporation of America (RCA). He then turned around and purchased KAO (Keith-Albee-Orpheum Theaters Corp.), a movie chain with 700 theaters in the US and Canada, with more than two million daily viewers. Kennedy then merged FBO with his chain of theaters (KAO) to form the famous RKO, and then had RCA trade its FBO stock for stock in the new company. He made a nice $2 million from the deal. Whether "Helene of Troy, N.Y." was ever distributed or survives from this company is still a mystery.

Helen appeared again during the 1950s-60s when poet Peter Viereck, one of the leading poets of the time, penned the following:

To Helen of Troy (N.Y.)
I sit here with the wind is in my hair;
I huddle like the sun is in my eyes,
I am (I wished you"d contact me) alone.
A fat lot you"d wear crape if I was dead.
It figures, who I heard there when I phoned you;
It figures, when I came there, who has went.
Dogs laugh at me, folks bark at me since then;
'she is," they say, "no better than she ought to;"
I love you irregardless how they talk.
You should of done it (which it is no crime)
With me you should of done it, what they say.
I sit here with the wind is in my hair.

Troy Chronicles

(Strict Form in Poetry: Would Jacob Wrestle with a Flabby Angel? Critical Inquiry, Vol 5. No 2 (Winter, 1978), pp. 203-222)

Ungrammatical perhaps, but hey, he's a poet. As he explained it: *"there is a double message: the denotative surface-rhythms tell us - with a grammatical error in very line - that this is a comic poem about a gross, crude, pathetic adolescent; the deeper connotative rhythms hint, in contrast, at a tragic poem about the wistful, delicate dignity of all wounded love."*

Helen appears again as recently as 1996. Carol Buck's book Love Goddesses (St. Martin's Press) contains three romances with each heroine having a name based on a historical figure. One of the short stories is titled "Myth and Magic: Helen of Troy, New York" and is written by Paula Detmer Riggs. This story is based on Helen Delorio from our city and her dealings with ex-husband and son.

The latest incarnation of Helen is from Greg Olear, a writer from Astoria who has penned a movie script entitled "Helen of Troy, N.Y." Greg and "Helen" were semifinalists in the Scriptapalooza Screenwriting Contest in 2001.

I asked Greg what his version of "Helen" was about and he replied: *"It's basically a modernization of the Helen of Troy story, set in Troy, N.Y., as a teen comic flick. She attends the private girls school there -- the name escapes me -- and is a conspiracy theorist. Paris, the hero, is on the photography team and goes to the public high school."*

Finally, I can report that I have actually found an off-Broadway troupe that performed the Kaufman-Connelly "Helen of Troy, N.Y." in 1986. I am now negotiating with them to bring the troupe to the Troy. It will be the first time "Helen" is played in her hometown, and I can"t think of a more appropriate thing to do than to bring a historic musical about our historic city to one of the most historic music halls in the country.

Troy Chronicles

NOTE: Justyna Kostek and I directed Helen of Troy, New York in Troy in 2014 to six sell out performances.

Frederick Proctor in 1905.

WILL TROY'S PROCTOR'S FINALLY BE SAVED

DID YOU KNOW?

1. FREDERICK PROCTOR BEGAN AS A POPULAR JUGGLER AND ACROBAT.

2. PROCTOR OWNED OVER A DOZEN THEATERS.

3. ALL THAT REMAINS OF HIS 1142-ACRE ESTATE IN CENTRAL VALLEY, NY IS THE GATEHOUSE. THE LAND AND BUILDINGS WERE PURCHASED BY THE US MILITARY ACADEMY AT WEST POINT FOR USE AS MILITARY AND PARACHUTE MANEUVERS AND ALL THE OTHER BUILDINGS WERE DESTROYED.

The Proctor's Theater in Troy was one of the last theaters built by the Vaudeville Giant Frederick Freeman Proctor in 1913-14, and was one of his most elegant creations. It has sat dormant for the last 30 plus years and several plans for redevelopment were introduced but none prevailed. This may be the last chance for the "Dean of Vaudeville's" prize monument.

Fred Proctor's story is the golden American story. The son of a rural doctor living in Maine he dreamed of being an acrobat and juggler wanting to run away and join the circus. He honed his skills while working for the famous R.H. White Dry Goods store in Boston and then joined with another juggler forming the Levantine Brothers Act. They made ten bucks a week. Later he joined with George E. Mansfield, who actually did run away from home and joined the circus. They were so good the team was earning $100 bucks a week traveling with the L.B. Lents Circus for more than five years.

Troy Chronicles

When Mansfield went to Europe alone Proctor went out on his own, but then decided to go to Europe too. There he toured with a fellow named Dan Busnell. Proctor used the stage name F.F. Levantine.

Proctor returned to America and settled in Albany looking for some engagements and worked for a small traveling circus that made the rounds in and around Albany. By the time he was 30 he saved up enough money to buy his own business and with $1000 dollars he purchased the old Green Street Theater on Green Street, later renaming it the Levantine's Theater and later the Gayety. This is the same theater that John Wilkes Booth and Joseph Henry performed in.

He did well and two years later bought the old Pearl Street Theater.

Proctor's often had lines around the block for movies.

Troy Chronicles

His first Albany Theater was called "Preeminently the Great Resort in Albany for Pleasurable Enjoyment."

Proctor went on to partner with Henry R. Jacobs when he came to town. Jacobs had made the 10, 20, 30 cents shows famous. The two of them revolutionized show business in America for the next seven years.

The team opened the Jacob and Proctors Museum on South Pearl and Beaver Street. First floor was stores, second floor a museum showing freaks, and the third was a theater.

In 1884 the Jacob and Proctor chain was created when they leased the Martin Opera House on South Pearl Street. Managers could book a whole season now and the two of them began starting theaters in every important city, including New York City, Philly and Chicago, where they had 3 or 4 houses each. Even during this partnership, Proctor maintained his own theaters. Eventually the two parted and Jacobs bought the Leland Opera House in Albany, and Proctor continued with the South Pearl Street establishment.
Front of Jacob and Proctor's Star Museum card.

In 1889 Proctor purchased

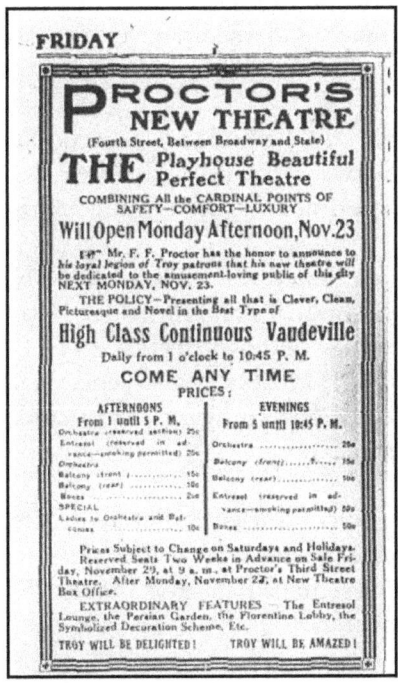

Proctor's ad announcing opening day.

the Leland from Jacob and turned it into a vaudeville house. Maurice Barrymore and Clara Morris, the first legitimate stars of the stage, played there.

It was Proctor who came up with the policy that no one could go into a theater without a ticket, a fact he learned when he tried to go into the Leland and the doorman wouldn't let him enter because he didn't know who he was. When he told him he was the owner, the doorman said sorry, he was told not to let anyone in without a ticket.

Ironically, even as Proctors built an empire he never built a theater in Albany; he only leased or purchased existing ones.

Proctors expanded into NYC in the late 1880s. By 1888 Proctor was managing 13 theaters and that now included the Griswold Opera House in Troy (located where the Atrium is today). Albany, however, was still the headquarters of the company.

In 1889, he built his first modern theater at 141 West 23rd St (Between 6th and 7th Avenues, NYC). He dubbed it "an experiment in high-grade legitimate productions."

He opened the Ladies Club Theater on 23rd street in 1892 and had 20 acts from 11 AM to 11PM. He had cards printed saying, "After breakfast go to Proctor's, After Proctor's go to bed." Mothers would send their children to the theater for the whole day knowing they would be safer there than on the street.

Proctor's Pleasure Palace on 58th built in 1895 was an experiment. This was a great amusement palace with amusement halls and theater. Even the roof had a garden theater.

In 1906 Proctor merged with B. F. Keith, the other giant in the business, and merged their NYC holdings. The Keith and

Interior of Troy Proctor's Theater.

Proctor's Theaters were impressive but Proctor sued in 1911 to end the relationship.

By 1912 moving pictures were gaining ground and Proctor was quick to incorporate the moving pictures and vaudeville, although he still felt vaudeville was king. The year 1915 is also the date that is often cited as the beginning of the decline of vaudeville. However Proctor's favorite motto was "Keep Plugging," and he did.

Proctor ended up controlling 16 theaters, with three in Albany and two in Troy. He even took out life insurance on his employees so that they didn't have to pay or worry about their families.

By 1928 Proctor had enough and he began selling off his holdings. In 1929 he sold his remaining 11 theaters to the Radio-Keith-Orpheum Corporation, basically a combo of RCA and vaudeville officials.

Troy Chronicles

In his heyday Proctor controlled 54 theaters around the country.

Locally he owned:

1880 Levantine's Novelty House, Green Street, Albany
1884 Martin's Opera House, Albany
1887 Griswold's Opera House, Troy
1889 Leland Opera House, Albany
1889 Proctor's Albany Theater
1904 Proctor's Annex Theater, N Pearl between maiden and Steuben Streets
1907 Proctor's State Street Theater, Schenectady
1909 Proctor's Theater, Cohoes
1912 The Lyceum, Troy
1913 Proctor's Grand Theater, Albany, corner Clinton and North Pearl Streets
1915 Proctor's Fourth Street Theater, Troy
1919 Proctor's Harmanus Bleecker Hall, Albany, Washington Avenue, south of Lark Street
1926 Proctor's New Theater, Schenectady

Only two theaters were built after the Troy Theater.

Proctor introduced many things: the ticket at the door, early bird matinee reduced admission price. He introduced a "fit for every purse," different price structures for box seats and other seating arrangements, and continuous runs. His theaters included bars, restaurants, and stores. His restaurants stayed open till 3 in the morning. He was the first to play a feature moving picture in a first class theater in 1912 when he played D.W. Griffith's Intolerance, a ten reel spectacular showing intolerance through the ages (perhaps it should be rereleased today). He was the first to introduce shared profits with employees. First to give his workers an interest in his business (many of his employees worked for 30 or 40 years for the company). He also pioneered the advertising trick of showing

Troy Chronicles

various theaters in a box form in an advertisement in the newspapers.

When Proctor died in 1929, he had 100 people in his will including a pastor in a small New England town that he learned was doing noble work with little funds, so he gave him a life income to carry on his work.

When Frederick F. Proctor designed this five-story entertainment complex in Troy in 1913-14, he wanted us to experience the outside and interior detail, and not just the performances of this original vaudeville house. This complex with theater and commercial space takes up most of the east side of Fourth Street between State Street and Broadway, and the facade of marble and terra cotta with lion heads and gargoyles is impressive today as it was on opening day. In the original design the upper level was suppose to have 23 apartments.

When workers tore down a false wall past the lobby a few years ago they were surprised by this 10-foot mural of Helen of Troy with ironworker and collar maid painted by David Lithgow.

Proctor's was billed as "Troy's Largest Amusement Place." Most of us "Little Italy" Catholics will remember the day at the theater when Jimmy Durante dedicated the opening of the new St. Anthony's School in the early "50s. Its voluminous space (seated over 2000 people) was designed as an entertainment space.

F.F. Proctor was class all the way and it is fitting that the Troy Theater is brought back to good use and a city hall in part of it would be fitting for a man who believed it serving his community.

The Common Council has expressed an interest in taking the commercial part of Proctor's and convert it to city hall. That's great thinking. The theater would be mothballed for now but hopefully given to a non-profit organization which can restore the theater. This has been done successfully throughout the country

In 2007 The Bethesda Cultural Alliance (Maryland) in 2007 reopened the newly renovated Bethesda Theatre. "This is a stunning example of all that can be accomplished when the public and private sectors work together," said John Slidell, president of the Bethesda Cultural Alliance. "We've worked since 1996 to breath new life into the theater, and thanks to the support of the state of Maryland and Montgomery County, the Bethesda Cultural Alliance has been able to see this project through and create a wonderful asset for the community."

The Bethesda Cultural Alliance, a nonprofit organization dedicated to the financial and operational support of the Bethesda Theatre, has worked closely with the state and county, along with private supporters, "The Bozzuto Group and Prudential" the restoration and reuse of the Bethesda Theatre. Not only will the theater provide off-Broadway performances, the Alliance also plans to use proceeds from the theater operation in support of local cultural arts activities.

Plans for renovating the Bethesda Theatre began in 1996 as part of The Bozzuto Group's development of The Whitney Apartments, located directly behind the theater. The Bozzuto Construction Company began restoring the Bethesda Theatre in 2001 under the direction of preservation architects. The theater's restoration has cost upwards of $11.75 million, which is a combination of private and public funds raised in part by the Bethesda Cultural Alliance.

In 2001, construction began to revitalize the Bethesda Theatre and apartments were built above and adjacent to the

Troy Chronicles

theatre. The Bethesda landmark building has been restored and in 2007 opens as a venue for live Off-Broadway theater.

There are hundreds of examples of historic theaters coming back to life championed by their communities: The Paramount Center for the Arts in Peekskill, the Capitol Theater in Port Chester. Tarrytown Music Hall, and the Port Chester 78-year-old Capitol Theater, and Irvington Town Hall Theater, to name a few.

There is also examples of how cities took the initiatives and did the restoration themselves, turning them into multipurpose venues that serve as a focal point for local arts and community activities. For example The Pix Theater in Lapper, Michigan (population 9,018) was built in 1941 but closed in the 1950s when TV became popular. It was purchased in 1996 by the Downtown Development Authority and restored in 1997. The private non-profit PIX Arts Council now manages the Theatre on behalf of the Downtown Development Authority offering approximately 50 live performances per season.

The city of Duluth Minnesota (population 86, 918) just purchased the historic NorShor Theatre and Temple Opera buildings in April. They spent $2.7 million for the complex.

There are other examples of successful restorations across the country. Let me direct you to Oakland's Paramount Theater that was purchased and restored In 1975 by the City of Oakland. The 1891 Fredonia (NY) Opera House, has been restored. "The Glove" is an 800 seat theatre in Gloversville and was restored. The New Amsterdam Theatre and Roundabout Theatre, Selwyn Theatre (now called the American Airlines Theatre) in New York City has been restored, Bardavon Opera House in Poughkeepsie has been restored, and The Little Theatre in Rochester is restored. All are other examples of communities that brought back their historic theaters. Why not Troy?

Troy Chronicles

Jacob Fabian began buying up theaters in the 1920s. He was operating Troy's Proctor's before 1935.

Proctor's represents one of the few examples of the earliest design of this genre that dominated the movie industry for about 50 years (from about 1910 through the 1960s). Theater architect John Eberson called movie palaces "the most palatial homes of princes and crowned kings for and on behalf of His Excellency the American Citizen."

In their heyday going to the movies was a way for the common folk to escape the drudgery of work and feel like royalty while doing it. Hollywood wanted us to feel special and they did whatever it took to make us feel that way. The largest picture palaces like the San Francisco Fox and the Roxy had a full-staffed hospital in case of emergencies. The Roxy's hospital staff (physicians, surgeons, and nurses) treated more than 12,000 patients in its male and female wards during the first year it was opened. Nurseries were available in most palaces; and in some, like the Loew's 72nd Street in New York City, they took care of your pets while you enjoyed the show.

Even the bathrooms were decorated for the rich including being staffed by attendants. When the famous Vanderbilt family demolished their Manhattan townhouse in the mid-1920s, Loew's bought much of the interior and had its workers dismantle their "Oriental Room" and bring it in pieces to Kansas City. It became the Women's Lounge of the Loew's Midland Theater in 1927. No, our Proctor's was not that elaborate but still there are many a Trojan who can tell of their first movie experience at Proctor's. Proctor's was one of those places in Troy that didn't care what social class you belonged to. The movies were open for everyone.

Proctor's was not built originally as a movie palace. It was actually built in 1913-14 for Vaudeville. Frederick F. Proctor's "New Theater." was promoted as having "Super Vaudeville,"

Troy Chronicles

and "Supreme Photo-Plays" and billed as "Troy's Largest Amusement Place." One of the earliest movie shows was Warner's, "The Mothers Penitent," a drama of the golden West. It premiered on February 2, 1914 and starred Baby Early and Elsie Albert. In 1917, Fred and Adele Astaire (before Ginger Rogers) appeared in person to "new songs and distinctive dance." I barely remember seeing Jimmy Durante there in the 50's when they were dedicating St. Anthony's School. Bob Hope played here, too.

Vaudeville and movies often shared the same stage. On November 9, 1929, you could see both Ruth Chatterton in "Once a Lady," and Rose's Midgets on the same bill at Proctors. Rose's "25 Lilliputians" were billed as "The Largest Company of Midgets In The World With the Only Midget Jazz Band." Quite a show, I bet.

By 1931, there were 11 theaters in our area offering such entertainment as Joan Crawford in "This Modern Age," Buster Keaton in "Sidewalks of New York," Eddie Cantor in "Palmy Days," or the double feature at the Palace showing Maurice Chevalier's "The Smiling Lieutenant" and Bert Wheeler's "Caught Plastered."

To build Proctor's the Bontecou, Gurley and Ide mansions on the east side of Fourth Street were torn down.

In 2003, the government estimated that the American public spent 12 billion dollars on the arts. It was also estimated that private donations to artists and arts organizations exceeded $12 billion, or $42 for each American. About half this total came from individuals, a third from foundations and the rest from corporations.

The arts are certainly an economic engine and if you look at Schenectady you can see the effects of it. The expansion of the other Proctor's Theater has brought Broadway plays to the city but also spinoff developments like restaurants and

Troy Chronicles

artists studios all in the immediate vicinity. Troy can have the same benefit if it decides to renovate Proctor's in Troy.

A report released recently by a consultant has concluded that Proctor's or the old telephone building could be chosen for the city's next city hall. The NY Telephone building is a new ugly building and no parking with the building. On the other hand, Proctor's with its history and memories from everyone over the age 50 (13.7% of the population is 65 or older) in the city, along with ample parking in the back is an ideal choice. The Common Council and city workers deserve to have a historic building for its offices. It has only had three city halls in its entire history and the last one was an eyesore. Give the theater to a non-profit organization who can then take the ball and run with it to restore the theater for multi use. As I said there are hundreds of examples throughout the country.

Proctor's has a very special place in the psyche of many Trojans. It isn't a former bank or department store. It is a space that many of us escaped our worries for a while. It's a place where we took our first love, our best friend, or to experience the thrill of a new movie, be it a love story, drama, sci-fi, or even a silly film about the Beatles. We even waited for hours in lines around the block. It was a place where others sang their first song, or performed their first act on stage. It was a place where you cried, laughed, or were scared silly. It was a place that carried as many emotions as there are seats. It would great if future generations could say the same thing.

Troy Chronicles

TWAS THE NIGHT BEFORE CHRISTMAS BEGAN IN TROY

Did You Know?

1. Moore did not admit to penning the poem until years after it was published.

2. The building where the poem was first published in Troy has a plaque on it but it is also the place where the fire of 1820 was stopped.

3. If Harriet Butler had not asked for a copy of the poem on a visit this now famous poem probably would never have seen the light of day.

Perhaps the most famous holiday poem ever is "Twas The Night Before Christmas" or as the author Clement Moore penned it, "A Visit from St. Nicholas." Many do not realize that there is a local connection to this poem.

Clement C. Moore, (1779-1863) was the son of Benjamin Moore, the president of Columbia College (have seen him associated with King's College as well) and second Protestant Episcopal Bishop of New York. Because of his financially secure background, he had donated 60 some acres of land in 1819 to establish the General Theological Seminary, where he taught several courses and authored the Compendious Lexicon of the Hebrew Language (the first ever). He was professor of Oriental and Greek Literature and Divinity and Biblical Learning at the Seminary.

Other historians have written that on Christmas Eve, 1822, his wife was roasting turkeys to feed the poor of the local parish but discovered that she was short one turkey. Like any good wife, she asked Moore to go get one. While riding "downtown" to Jefferson Market (now the Bowery section), Moore composed the poem while riding in his sleigh. He returned with the turkey and a poem and after dinner Moore read the poem to his family and his kids loved it. Moore was a respected educator and writer and so would not admit to penning such a frivolous poem.

Moore's father, the bishop, previously had christened the new St. Paul's Episcopal Church on Third Street in Troy that was headed by the Reverend David Butler. Butler, who was born in Harwinton, Connecticut on July 19, 1762, had served in

Clement Moore.

Troy Chronicles

the Connecticut Line of the American Army during the latter months of the Revolution. In 1792, he was ordained Deacon by the Right Rev Samuel Seabury in Trinity Church, New Haven, Connecticut, and also ordained him as a on Priest on June 19, 1793, at Middletown, Connecticut. He served as rector of several Connecticut churches in Litchfield, Reading, Danbury, and Ridgefield and in 1805 was instituted as rector of the parishes of Troy and Lansingburgh staying with the Troy parish of St. Paul's Church until his death on July 11, 1842.

Butler and Moore knew each other and visited each other's families. On one occasion, Butler's daughter Harriet visited the New York City Moore family and heard Rev. Moore recite the poem to his kids. She asked for a copy of it and gave it to Orville L. Holley, editor of the Troy Sentinel on River Street. On December 23, 1823, the poem was published for the first time but anonymously. We do not know if that was done because Harriet asked or if the editor made that choice. Often during that time, poems were published with the author's initials only, however, it has been written that Moore, upon learning of the publication was not happy about its publication considering ownership would be too frivolous for such a pious man of the cloth.

It wasn't until 1829 that Moore's name was hinted in the Troy Sentinel stating it belonged by birth and residence to the City of New York, and that he is a gentleman of more merit as a scholar and writer than many of more noisy pretentions." The following year, Myron King, a wood engraver in Troy illustrated the poem with Santa Claus with sleigh and reindeer riding over housetops for the 1830 edition of the Sentinel. In 1837, The New York Book of Poetry was published and included the poem without Moore's name but on December 25, 1838 in issue of the Troy Budget newspaper, Moore was cited as the author for the first time. He would not admit to it until 1844 at age 65 (he was 43 when he wrote it) when he published a book of his own poetry.

Troy Chronicles

In the meantime, the poem has been parodied more than Moore would have wanted for sure, and I'm the first to admit guilt. When I was writing my history column for the Troy Record back at the turn of the century, I penned a few but you have to be a Trojan to get them. You can try here:

Dec 16, 2003
http://www.donrittner.com/his233.html
Dec 24, 2002
http://www.donrittner.com/his184.html
Dec 25, 2001
http://www.donrittner.com/his136.html

There is some controversy over whether Moore actually wrote the poem or it was penned by Henry Livingston, a Dutchman.

Copy of the original poem by Moore, page one. Only four exist. Source: Internet at http://www.clementcmoore.com/

Chapter Five
MUSIC

MANHATTAN TRANSFER AND THE TROY CONNECTION

DID YOU KNOW?

1. TIM'S BOYHOOD HOME IS NOW VACANT.

2. MANHATTAN TRANSFER CONTINUES TO ENTERTAIN FANS EACH YEAR.

3. TIM HAS HIS OWN PODCASTS ON HIS WEB PAGE AT HTTP://TIMHAUSERMUSIC.COM WHERE YOU CAN ALSO ORDER HIS HOMEMADE PASTA SAUCE.

Tim Hauser is best known as a singer and originator of Manhattan Transfer, a popular singing group that he formed in 1969. They are known for their great harmonies and classy dress and today the band is in the form of Tim, Cheryl Bentyne, Janis Siegel and Alan Paul. They continue to produce quality music and perform around the world.

Tim's first version of Manhattan Transfer began in 1969 with Gene Pistilli, Marty Nelson, Erin Dickins and Pat Rosalia and they produced one album called Jukin (Capitol Records) that leaned more towards a country/R&B sound. Since Tim was more interested in jazz and swing the band went their separate ways in the early 70s.

Troy Chronicles

Manhattan Transfer. Tim on left. Photo by Tim Hauser.

Tim continued singing and driving a taxi to make a living until he reformed the group in 1972 with Laurel Masse, Janis Siegel and Alan Paul. It was the taxi driving that had a hand in forming the new group. He met Masse while driving cab picking her up after her stint as a waitress and finding out they had a mutual interest in music. The cab ride was also responsible for finding Janis Siegel after he picked up the Congo player for Laurel Canyon who invited Tim to a party. Fellow Laurel Canyon member Seigel was in attendance. Again they struck up a friendship and shared a mutual interest in music. Finally, Masse's boyfriend suggested to Tim that a fourth and male voice was needed and to check out

Troy Chronicles

Photo by Tim Hauser.

Alan Paul who was then in the Broadway cast of "Grease." On October 1, 1972 the new Manhattan Transfer was formed.

Their album in 1975 produced the hit "Operator" giving them national recognition. That same year Manhattan Transfer had a summer replacement hour-long TV show on Sunday night at 8 PM occupying the former original Ed Sullivan hour.

Masse left the group while recovering from a car accident in 1978 and was replaced by Soprano Cheryl Bentyne in 1979. Her first performance was debuted on their album Extensions which produced another hit Twilight Zone/Twilight Tone. It also featured Birdland and the group won two Grammy Awards for the album.

Since then Tim's group has won 8 other Grammys (12 nominations). Tim served on the original voting committee of the Rock and Roll Hall of Fame for the first three years (1986-88). Tim released a solo album in 2007 called Love Stories which you can purchase and download from his web site. He currently lives in California and his own website (besides the official Manhattan Transfer site) is at http://timhausermusic.com/. Tim is also famous for his sauce and sells it commercially. It is known as "I Made Sauce." I need to find a local distributor for that one. Would be good with the homemade pasta from the Schenectady Greenmarket. Hmm, maybe I can do a trade.

However, as Paul Harvey use to say now for the rest of the story. Tim was born five days after the Japanese bombed

Troy Chronicles

Pearl Harbor in Troy, N.Y. on December 12, 1941.
The year before developer Frank Gunderson had just built six brand new houses on Schuyler Drive in Wynantskill. The street was still dirt and nothing surrounded the new neighborhood when newborn Tim became the newest member of the Hauser family who resided at number one Schuyler Drive. Like Jack and Terry Hauser's, the other homes were filled with young couples like Dot and Jack Liberty, the Nimmens and Bookheims, but It was a challenging time for America as we were entering the second world war. Tim remembers fondly of the childhood neighborhood, in particular, when his dad took him out in the dark because he left his toys outside or being scared to death by "Ah Ooga," the sounds of an old horn on a Model T belonging to the neighbor who lived behind him.

Tim's boyhood home on Schuyler taken in 1941 five months after Tim was born. Photo by Tim Hauser.

Tim's dad who had a chronic heart condition could not go overseas but instead served in the Civil Air Patrol to do his part for the war effort. Tim told me that he believes it always bothered his dad that he could not go overseas because his brother Lincoln Dapron became a big hero in the Pacific Theater and a book was written about him and others titled "An American Guerrilla in the Philippines" (Ray C. Hunt and Bernard Norlinc, 1986, University Press of Kentucky). A movie was also made of it in 1950 (American Guerrilla in the Philippines) starring Tyrone Power and directed by Fritz Lang of Metropolis fame. Tim's dad's stepfather Dr. Louis Hauser

Troy Chronicles

Tim in his sandbox on Maple Ave. Photo by Tim Hauser.

was a Navy medical officer on the Missouri when the Japanese signed the instruments of surrender. When Tim was two years old the family moved to 63 Collins Avenue, the street that runs parallel to Pinewoods Ave in East Albia, in a duplex where they lived downstairs. Tim recalls the old Crescent Cleaners that was behind them and the days he would stand on the back porch listening to the sounds of the pressing machines on a cold day.

In 1945 they moved around the corner to 126 Maple Avenue close to Emma Willard School. His mom use to bring him to Emma Willard during Christmas to listen to the girls sing. Tim attended the Sacred Heart Church on Sundays and remembers how beautiful the old Vanderheyden Orphanage buildings were. Tim and his next door neighbor, June, often took tin cans and tied string between them and talk to each across the driveway (my friend Paul Kink and I did that too).

He also remembers an event that was funny to him and not so funny to his dad. His father and his Uncle Steve took Tim and June to Crescent Cleaners one day to pick up clothes in his 1938 Ford two-door sedan. When his dad got in the car the back of the seat broke and he fell all the way back. Tim began laughing but his dad turned around and smacked him. Tim learned the limits of his father's sense of humor. I can relate to that. The only time my father hit me was when I burned the ribbons off his medals from the war. Pretty touchy I thought at the time!

Down the street towards Collins Avenue was Mrs. Dunsback and her favorite pies, a big hit in the neighborhood. Tim use to bring the pie tins back to her and would bang them against his knee on the way, developing a beat coordination that he would certainly use later in life. He attended preschool at Maple Avenue and remembers an incident where kids had ringworm with large patches shaved on their heads with iodine on them. He later attended PS 16 on Collins Avenue until it burned. Tim would often visit the Liberty's who also moved at the same time to East Albia from Schuyler Street. One of the sons, named Hugh (Huey), built balsa wood model fighter planes (my cousin Dave did that too) and hang them on the ceiling. Tim would sit in Huey's bedroom and just stare at the planes hanging on the ceiling thinking they were cool. My cousin Dave and I tried to shoot his down with a rocket launcher. Ah the joys of being young boys!

Tim's Collins Avenue home now is vacant. Photo by Tim Hauser.

Tim also has a reason to believe in Santa Claus. His bedroom was in the back facing the backyard and directly under his window was the roof of the shed where his dad kept his tools. There was a heavy snow on Christmas Eve in 1945 and Tim woke up early on Christmas morning excited as any

Troy Chronicles

young boy would be on that day. On his bed was a large stocking filled with toys. When the morning became brighter he looked out the window and saw in the snow footprints that ran across the yard to the shed and on the roof of the shed right by his window. He knew Santa had made a visit. Ironically, it was the Christmas that celebrated the end of the war. His parents took Tim downtown to watch the big parade in Troy celebrating the war's end and his dad marched in the parade.

Tim's dad worked for Behr Manning Paper Company in 1940 and was a semi-pro baseball player pitching left handed for their team. He also worked for Pioneer Savings Bank but even though the owner of the bank saw a future for him, he did not want to become a banker so he opened the South Lake Ave Lumber Company, off Hoosick Street, and he and his partners made wooden pallets. His dad would take Tim in his blue '37 Ford truck to Vermont to pick up lumber from the mills and he recalls what a beautiful ride it was. Route 7 is still a great ride today.

After the war and inflation, his father's business collapsed. They were wiped out. His Uncle Steve (Stephen Butters) who lived across the street during the Wynantskill days was in the Battle of the Bulge, shot in the hand, and ended up in General Eisenhower's SHAPE headquarters interrogating captured German officers. Tim says that German was spoken fluently in the family. Like many war stories, when

Tim in his 1939 Ford! He restored a 1940 Mercury Convertible Coup. Courtesy of Tim Hauser.

Troy Chronicles

Steve came back from the war he found his wife had left him for another and he moved to Asbury Park, NJ as a photographer. It was Uncle Steve who convinced Tim's dad to move to New Jersey and they moved lock stock and barrel and said goodbye to Troy to start a new life. The rest of the story is of course history. When Tim performs nearby he often visits the old neighborhoods and loves to return to Troy where he still has some friends to visit. I envision (and hope) that Manhattan Transfer one day will be performing at the new restored Proctor's Theater on 4th Street. I haven't told Tim about that yet!!!!

NOTE: Tim died on October 16, 2014.

Tim's Maple Avenue home is still occupied and owned by a family that enjoys the music of Manhattan Transfer. Photo by Don Rittner.

FRANKIE CARLE AND THE TROY BROTHEL

DID YOU KNOW?

1. BIG BANDS FOUGHT WITH EACH OTHER TO HIRE CARLE.

2. DURING WORLD WAR II HE MADE $1,000 A WEEK AND 5% OF THE GROSS.

3. ALTHOUGH THE 1940S WERE THE HIGH POINTS OF HIS CAREER HE CONTINUED TO PLAY DURING THE 1980S; THAT'S OVER 70 YEARS OF PLAYING.

Frankie Carle, one of the biggest big band leaders of the 40's had a hit song called Sunrise Serenade. It could be heard on the "A" side of Benny Goodman's Moonlight Serenade recorded in 1939 on the Bluebird label.

It was Carle's biggest hit and signature song that rose to Number One in the nation in 1938, selling more than a million copies. Other hits to his credit, included "Carle Boogie," "Lover's Lullaby," "Sunrise in Napoli", "Dream Lullaby," and "Oh, What It Seemed To Be," made popular by Frank Sinatra. He had several hits with his daughter, singer Marjorie Hughes, such as "A Little On the Lonely Side," "Rumors Are Flying" and "It's All Over Now."

The real story about Sunrise Serenade is that it was written in Troy, N.Y. Carl was working at the Clock House, a brothel at the time. Other Troy locations he played were the Showboat and the Paradise, a gambling boat that was parked out on the Hudson near Fulton Street but sunk in the flood of 1936.

Troy Chronicles

Frankie Carle. Wikipedia.

The story goes that Carl was up all night composing music and someone called the police because of all the noise. The cops told him to cut out the sunrise serenade so he ended up naming the tune just that. He teamed up with lyricist Jack Lawrence who wrote the words. According to Lawrence:

"I had made a good reputation as a facile lyric writer of songs that first came to notice as instrumentals, such as "In an 18th Century Drawing Room." This intriguing instrumental written by Frankie Carle first came to prominence in a Glen Gray Casa Loma Orchestra recording. Lou Levy tipped me off to this forthcoming hit and despite the fact that he was not its publisher, he arranged for me to meet Frankie who was appearing with his own band somewhere in the Boston area.

Frankie, who'd been knocking around the music business for quite a few years, was overwhelmed by his sudden success. I suggested some modifications in his melody so that it would be sing-able and he agreed. Both as an instrumental and vocal we got a slew of recordings and kept the number one spot on the Hit Parade for many months."

Fact or Fiction?
Either way, you can listen to some of Carl's hits at
http://www.archive.org/details/FrankieCarlOrchestra

Or on Youtube
http://www.youtube.com/artist/Frankie_Carle

Chapter Six
THE LAW

TROY'S EARLY LAW & ORDER

DID YOU KNOW?

1. ALBERT PAWLING WAS APPOINTED THE COUNTY'S FIRST SHERIFF AND LATER BECAME MAYOR OF TROY.

2. THE FIRST LAW OFFICER IN THE TROY AREA WAS JACOB PLANK, WHO WAS SHERIFF OF RENSSELAERWYCK IN 1634.

3. TROY'S "NIGHT WATCH" BEGAN IN 1789.

Our first established system of criminal law dates back to 2500 BC with the Code of Hammurabi, but it was the Romans that created the first organized police force, the Roman Vigile, created by Gaius Octavius, the grand nephew of Julius Caesar. The very word "police" however is derived from the Greek word 'Polis' meaning city.

In North America, policing obviously wasn't employed until Europeans first settled here. Boston is believed to be the first to establish a "Night Watch" in April 1631, comprising part time officers serving for no pay. Our region was close behind. In Albany in 1634, Jacob Planck became a "Schout" for the Colonie of Rensselaerwyck. While his duties were mostly judicial and administrative, he had policing powers as well. That was followed in 1652 when Evert Brantsen was appointed undersheriff of Beverwyck (the village of Albany) in December 1652, the same year Beverwyck was formed. In 1675 constables were chosen to create a watch. In 1652, New Amsterdam (New York City) established a Rattle Watch, where patrolmen communicated to one another by shaking little wooden rattles using a series of 10 codes. Albany also had a rattle watch in the 1670's and perhaps earlier. Albany also had a horse guard, a mounted police. By 1712, Boston had a full time paid law enforcement.

In Troy, none of that existed since Troy did not become a village until 1787, but it didn't take long. On September 24, 1789, the village of Troy created the first "Night Watch" and hired four constables. In 1791, Albert Pawling was appointed first Rensselaer County sheriff, and the first Constables were elected in the Village of Troy: David Henry, William Hikok, Laurence Dorsit, and Samuel Colamore. Pawling would later become Troy's first mayor.

The duties of the Night Watch were to patrol the quiet streets of the village, and cry, 'all's well!' at the expiration of each hour. When a building was discovered to be on fire, the loud cry of 'fire! fire!' aroused the inhabitants and the firemen. When the fire was extinguished, those returning from it cried, 'All out! All out!'

When Troy incorporated in 1816, the police force consisted of six constables who were elected annually. The cost of maintaining the 'City Watch' was seven hundred and sixty-four dollars and eighty-one cents according to the report of the first Chamberlain.

Troy Chronicles

It was also part of the duty of the Watchmen of the City in 1816 to pick up the firebuckets left at a fire and bring them back to the markethouse within twelve hours after such fire had been extinguished.

In the year 1829, the police force of Troy consisted of a 'High Constable' and six constables. Revilo Clark was High Constable and his subordinates were Lewis G. Dole, Justin Kellogg, Ezra Moseley, John Burtis, Jr., William Follett, Lyman J. Rundell. Daniel H. Stone was Police Justice.

In 1830, the force of constables was increased by the addition of four 'Special Constables:' John Prescott, John Bulmson, Lewis G. Dole, and Joseph C. Vaughan. The regular constables were William Y. Wilson, Robert Martin, Ezra Moseley, Martin Russell, William Follett, Edward Lyons. Gad Dumbolton was High Constable and George Butler, Chief Justice.

In 1833, the system of Ward Constables went into effect. Each ward had its own constable. The Ward Constables then were Elam N. Buel, Robert Martin, Ezra Moseley, Elisha Lovett, William Follett and Martin Russell, who represented the six separate wards respectively. In addition there were four Special Constables.

One year later an office of Public Crier and Bellman was created. John Lawrence and Sheldon Morris served. It was part of their duty to give the alarm should occasion arise.

It wasn't until 1851 that a Night Police Force was organized in Troy, but as you will learn in that getting a professional police force organized in Troy had some serious bumps and grinds along the way.

Four members of the Capital District regional police department in 1860. Names unknown.

Troy Chronicles

TROY'S FIRST "COPPS"

DID YOU KNOW?

1. THE TERM "COP" IS ATTRIBUTED TO TROY'S FIRST POLICE CHIEF, AMASA COPP.

2. TROY AND LANSINGBURGH HAD THEIR OWN SEPARATE POLICE DEPARTMENTS.

3. FROM 1865 TO 1870 TROY DID NOT HAVE A POLICE FORCE BUT WAS PART OF THE CAPITAL DISTRICT POLICE FORCE.

Troy's first law enforcement was a series of hired, and then, elected constables that served the wards of the new emerging city. In 1851, the city established a Night Police Force. The Night Force Committee of the Common Council had the ultimate authority of this force acting as one police superintendent and consisted of Alderman Alexander Halstead (7th ward), Hiram Smith (3rd Ward) and Winant Bennett (6th Wad). They hired Amasa Copp as the first chief. Copp was popular and the now often used slang "Cop" is attributed to him.

Photo by Lloyd.   TIMOTHY QUINN,
Chief of the Night Police, 1859-1860

Troy's first group of policemen belonging to this new night force was Henry Campbell, John Symonds, and Edgar Allen. The rest of the list was George Capron, Valentine Geist. James Delany, James Murphy, James Carson, Patrick Clifford, Calvin Green, William B. Campbell,

Troy Chronicles

Michael Mahon, Daniel McAdams, Thomas L. Ayres, Charles Allen, Michael Guy, John Austin, Thomas Sayles, William Taplin, William Flack, Dennis Glennon, Richard Green, Jr., Samuel Place, Thomas K. Murray, Alexander Wheeler, Samuel Edmondson, Patrick Ryan, Patrick Regan, John O'Brien, Henry McGrath, William H. Bonesteel, Patrick Casey, James H. Ballard, William Wallace, Joseph Mostyn, John Tomey, Simon Swartwout, Royal C. Levings, John Lockwood, Michael Quinn. Elbridge G. Wellington, Henry Lowell, Michael Brennon, Lorenzo D. Ford, Spencer Hulbert, Frederick Bonesteel, Edwin R. Smith, Peter Roberts. Backups or supernumeraries were William Holmes, Richard Tobin, John Higgins, Daniel Agan, William Noonan, Hugh Horrigan, Joseph Linmer, Robert Rogers, Sidney Wright, Peter Lavine, Kerun Egan, and Stephen Duffy.

In 1851, the number of wards of Troy increased when the sixth ward was divided into the sixth and ninth wards, and the seventh ward into the tenth and seventh wards. In 1854, the Night Police Force was subdivided into three squads. The salary of the Chief of the Night Police was fixed at four hundred dollars a year in 1857. Copp was replaced with Timothy Quinn as Chief of the Night Police in 1859 and the police headquarters set at 99 First Street. Each of the three divisions

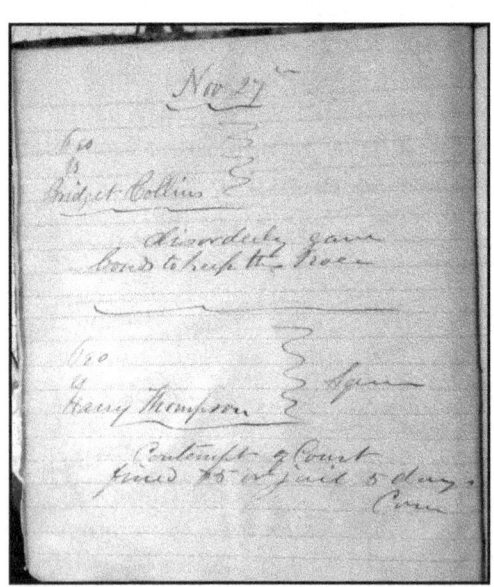

Arrest record during the reign of the Capital Police Force in Troy on November 27, 1867

of the force had a Roundsman. Michael Guy, Charles H. Cleavland and Thomas H. Peck were the first Roundsmen.

At the beginning of the Civil War in 1861, the Force was divided into three divisions, with about twenty-five members each. The first captains of these divisions were Charles R. Squire, James C. Moss and Jacob M. Wood. The following year a detective division was created and headquartered at 86 Second Street. There were two members, Walter L. Kipp and Lemuel Hurlburt.

Where did prisoners go when arrested? The first county jail was erected in 1793 on the SW corner of the alley behind the first Court House, located basically the same as it is today. The jail was a two-story brick building.

A whipping-post and a pair of stocks were placed in the Court House yard in 1795. John Weden was the first man to be publicly whipped for horse stealing. On Saturday evening, November 14, 1795, he received forty lashes in the presence of a large crowd.

In 1826, a new brick jail was built on the NW corner of Ferry Street and Fifth Avenue with a capacity of 126 prisoners. On Tuesday afternoon, January 28, 1845, William Miller, a German, was the first to be hung in the jail for the murder of George West, a German resident of Sandlake. The execution took place in the upper hall of the jail where gallows had been erected, in front of the Sheriff and about fifty citizens.

The police force was doing a suitable job by all measures but this was to change in 1865, when the legislature passed the Capitol Police District Act in 1865. It abolished all police forces in Troy, Albany, Bethlehem, the villages of West Troy, Green Island, and Cohoes, the village of Lansingburgh, and the towns of North Greenbush and Greenbush, and within the County of Schenectady, all that territory covered by and included within the lines of property of the New York

Central Railroad between the cities of Albany and Schenectady. This area was united into one Capital Police Force.

The Capital Police Force was composed of a Superintendent, a Deputy Superintendent, Captains of Capital Police, Sergeants and Patrolmen. Three Commissioners and Two Advisory Commissioners were appointed by the Governor on the passage of the act, who were the chief officers of the Capital Police. One Commissioner and one Advisory Commissioner had to reside in the city of Troy, and one Commissioner and one Advisory Commissioner in the city of Albany. Their term of office was six years. This system of successful policing lasted for only five years, and was abolished on April 29, 1870. Troy and Lansingburgh would immediately get their own police departments back.

Troy Chronicles

DOUBLE TROUBLE IN '82

DID YOU KNOW?

1. TWO POLICE DEPARTMENTS IN THE SAME CITY IS A FORMULA FOR DISASTER.

2. CRIMINALS WHO WERE ARRESTED WERE CLAIMED BY BOTH FORCES AND FIGHTS BROKE OUT.

3. THE NEW POLICE FORCE TRIED TO RAID THE OLD POLICE PRECINCTS.

Troy has many unique stories regarding its 200-year history, but none as interesting as the period in which it had two different police forces at the same time. The year 1882 was not a good year for criminals, or both police forces that spent as much time arresting each other as they did common criminals.

Naturally, it all began with politics! Blame it on the Troy Common Council. It occurred during the first administration of Mayor Edmund Fitzgerald, in 1882. It seems that a dispute arose as to the legality of Alderman James Morrissey's election to the Board of Aldermen for the 7th ward. The Democratic members of the board, objecting to the outcome of the vote, decided to get up in a huff and leave a council meeting believing that without them no business would be conducted. Bad move, boys! The Republican and independent members of the council got together and chose a new board of police commissioners consisting of Elisha Hydorn, John Magill, and Samuel Craig.

It was Commissioner Craig who became the center of the problem. It seems even his election was disputed and so Craig removed the existing Superintendent John McKenna and

Troy Chronicles

installed John Quigley as head of the police department. Quigley soon realized that none of the members of the police force would obey his orders. The patrolmen and even their superior officers pledged their loyalty to Superintendent McKenna, who they claimed to be their real chief officer.

The feud ended up in court where it remained for over a year. Pending a court decision, Quigley filed charges against the officers and patrolmen who ignored his orders, and those men were found guilty of insubordination by the Police Board and 'removed' from the force on November 21, 1882. ‚Ä®The heads of the precincts, Captains Patrick McCarthy (First), Coleman O'Loughlin (Second), and John McGrath (Third) were then replaced by John O'Connor who was made Captain of the First, D. J. Cary, Captain of the Second and George Gorman, Captain of the Third Precinct. The original detectives, Cornelius Markham, Edward J. McKenna, Bernard Roarke and Charles R. Squire, were replaced with Michael Flynn, John H. Campbell, and John O. Hairn and Fred C. Rogers.

There was one major hitch to the whole situation. None of the members of the old force recognized their dismissal and in fact kept their uniforms and equipment. More importantly, they kept control of the various precinct houses as well as main Police Headquarters.

The new Police Force established alternative headquarters in the basement of City Hall and made attempts (raids?) to get control of the precincts. However, they were constantly kept barricaded by the members of the old force. Even fights broke out, and on one instance eleven members of the new force were "arrested" by the old force and put in jail cells - under lock and key. Unfortunately for criminals, both police forces competed with each other in arresting those that broke the law, and in fact many criminals were claimed by both. Not a good year to be a criminal in the "collared" city!

Troy Chronicles

This situation went on for 14 months, between 1882-83, before the Court of Appeals finally handed down a decision in favor of the new police force, and the old force capitulated. Since they served 14 months with no pay, they presented claims to recover their wages, and a compromise was reached with the city and they received about half pay.

To insure this didn't happen again a new law was passed on March 13, 1885, titled "An Act to Increase the Police Force of the City of Troy, to Reorganize the Same and to Reorganize the Board of Police Commissioners." It provided for the appointment of two Police Commissioners of opposite political views by the President of the Common Council. Terms of office were two years, and the additional appointment of two other Police Commissioners, whose term of office were four years, were added. Samuel Craig, John Magill, James Fleming, and Elisha W. Hydorn were chosen as commissioners. Fleming was the compromise. A new police force was formed and William W. Willard was made Superintendent of Police to succeed John Quigley, and new patrolmen were hired. Many of the members of the old force originally removed by the Police Commissioners under Mayor Fitzgerald, received their old jobs back.

The moral of the story for the city council? Work together for the good of all Trojans and leave the sour grapes for wine making.

Troy Chronicles

"COMMUNITY POLICE" NOT NEW

DID YOU KNOW?

1. LANSINGBURGH HAD ITS OWN POLICE FOR 30 YEARS BEFORE TROY WAS CREATED.

2. THE LANSINGBURGH PRECINCT STATION HOUSE STILL EXISTS ON SECOND AVENUE AND HAS THE WORDS POLICE OVER THE DOOR.

3. THE SOUTH TROY POLICE STATION WAS BUILT BY THE WPA (WORKS PROGRESS ADMINISTRATION) IN 1935 AND STILL SURVIVES NEXT TO THE FIRE STATION PAST CANAL STREET.

There has been much talk lately about the "new" community police force taking shape in the Burgh. Ironically, the village of Lansingburgh was policing its own for 30 years before Troy ever saw a building lot.

The village had a series of non-uniformed watchmen and constables until all the police departments were organized into the uniformed Capital Police Force in 1865. After the Capital Police system was abolished in 1870, the village instituted its own police force in 1871 under the jurisdiction of a Board of Police Commissioners and a Captain of Police. Alexander King was Captain.

The village police department worked out of one station house, although it had several locations. First located on Second Avenue, between Seventeenth and Eighteenth Streets in the McMurray building, they then moved to the Noyes building on Seventeenth Street. On September 1, 1898, they moved operations into 606 Second Avenue. They continued working here until the village was annexed and it then became the Fourth Precinct house. When it opened in 1898, it was touted to have the latest amenities: electric lights, four steel cells, fire alarm striker and burglar alarms that connected with the Peoples' Bank and the bank of D. Powers and Son, both located nearby. Captain Morris E. Kirkpatrick was in command of the precinct from 1896 until 1900, when the village was annexed to Troy under the act providing for second-class cities.

The Capital Police Force Manuel of Operation. Photo by Don Rittner.

There were three wards in the Burgh and 13 patrolmen served the village. The village was stunned with the murder of Patrolman Mosher Burnham on October 23, 1881. He was found in an alley between Fourth and Fifth Avenues, south of Twentieth Street and had been shot through the abdomen. It took several years to find the murderer.

When the 20th century rolled into Troy, on January 1, 1900, there were four police precincts in the city with less than 100 patrolmen. General offices for the Department were on the first floor at City Hall on the corner of Third Street and State Street (now Barker Park), until 1926, while the precinct stations were located in key locations throughout the city.

Troy Chronicles

The First Precinct Station house was located at the corner of Third Street and Canal Avenue (now a park) and was built in 1893. Its boundaries were "all south of Liberty Street, to Greenbush line, lying between the Hudson River and east bounds of the city, including the 8th, 11th, 9th, 12th, and 6th wards." The WPA built a new precinct house next to the firehouse on the east side of Third Street in 1935. The building is now privately owned.

The Second Precinct Station house was located at 22 State Street (demolished) and was built in 1872. Its boundaries included the "North side of Liberty Street to center line of Federal Street, lying between the Hudson River and east bounds of the city, including the 1st, 2and, and 3rd wards, and that part of the 4th ward lying south of center line of Federal Street and that portion of the 5th and 14th wards lying between the Poestenkill and a line drawn through center of Federal Street and same produced eastwardly."

The Third Street Precinct Station House was located 2420 Fifth Avenue (demolished) and was built in 1876. Its boundaries were "All north of Federal Street to former Lansingburgh line, and from the Hudson River to the east bounds of the city, embracing part of the 4th ward and the 7th, 10th, and 13th and a part of the 14th wards."

The Fourth Precinct included the entire Burgh. The precinct house is now a saloon.

On June 14, 1905, a plan was submitted for a Fifth Precinct, in east side, but didn't materialize. By 1914, the precinct stations were rundown and on June 6, the city was served with a show cause order by the State Prison Commission to show why the First, Second, and Third Precinct Station houses shouldn't be demolished and rebuilt. The three station houses were actually condemned by the commission, and it wasn't until June 2, 1921, that the city engineer proposed the consolidation of the precincts into one central station. The fourth precinct station was declared in good shape.

In 1926-27, the Second and Third Precincts were consolidated into the newly built Central Police Precinct at 55 State Street. A new First Precinct Station house was built on the east side of Second Street adjacent to the Fire House in 1935. Finally in 1944, the First and Fourth Precincts were absorbed into the Central Police Precinct so that all operations of the force were conducted out of one building, except for the 1920-built signal station house next door. Currently, there are plans to renovate the central police station on State Street.

www.ingramcontent.com/pod-product-compliance
Lightning Source LLC
Chambersburg PA
CBHW022153080426
42734CB00006B/416